Library of Congress Control Number: 2023906308

FOUR HOURS WITH JESUS

Based on a True Story

Cindy Medlock

All the events in this memoir are true to the best of the author's memory. The views expressed in this memoir are solely those of the author.

My deepest gratitude is to God for His provision and guidance and for putting me into a support system that only He knew how much I needed.

A very special thank you to all of those who helped me when I was struggling as a single mother. My wonderful church family at Lithia Christian Center in Georgia (which in recent years was sold and the original church is now in Dallas, Georgia, going by the name "The Church at the Well"). I can never thank you enough for being there for me and my children. You truly are saints! Thank you for showing me the love of Christ at a time when I so desperately needed it. Blessings and honor to you for your dedication to the community and to all those you have helped and nurtured in Christ. I think of you often and always with much reverence.

God bless you for the music ministry that lifted me up when I didn't feel I could go on. You will never truly know the impact you have had…well, maybe you will in heaven. A special thank-you to Ms. Barbara, my loving mentor, and her dear sister, Ms. Bunnie, the pastor's wife, who administered the many programs on the campus.

Thank you to my parents who helped me financially with attorney fees and other expenses, and to my dad for coming to my court proceedings when I so needed social support. Thank you to my parents for teaching me the Word of God and showing me Christ at an early age. I believe it's the greatest thing a parent can do for the eternal well-being of a child.

When we stand before the Lord to give an account of our lives, our partner won't be beside us. So, it's always important to have our identity come from Christ, not jobs, partners, houses, or lands, but Him alone. I know this because I totally lost my identity in my marriage. Everything was about pleasing my husband and not my Savior. But just time alone with the Savior each day can make such an impact. Life is uncertain, even though we often refuse to believe bad things could be in our future. A spouse can represent that uncertainty. For example, he or she may not always be available, trustworthy, or a reliable provider.

Thank you to my helpers and editors, Dr. John Monagin, MD and Kristi Thomas. This book would not have been possible without the help of these two dear friends.

Table of Contents

Introduction

This is a story of a woman so downtrodden she could hardly think her way out of her terrible situation, yet it was only by the grace of God that she could, with persistent effort and dedication, escape to a better life.

Serving the Lord is not an easy path. Yet thinking of others and even doing small favors for someone in need not only causes them to feel better but also makes the person who reached out feel better.

Thus, honoring your Maker and following His injunctions to treat one's neighbor as you would treat yourself (crucial advice in Luke 10) makes for a respectful and rewarding experience. To ignore the needs of others or pretend you just didn't even notice is the work of a petty soul and a missed opportunity. Multiple events can accrue over time and add up, ultimately, to a rather meaningless life. Yet many people get drawn into such lifestyles, feeling that if they avoid criminal activity or grossly harming others, they're doing just fine.

Often people believe that doing good things in the world is readily done and no great burden. And when helping others is inconvenient or personally difficult that too can feel fulfilling yet exact a price in everyday life. And then there are smaller and more subtle favors we can do for others and ourselves, which only we may be aware of, such as avoiding superficiality or maliciously judging others; daily challenges for all of us.

If the Lord tested His children in many ways in the Scripture, and He is an unchanging God, should we not expect that He tests us today? I believe He does, as He certainly did with me. Did Abraham tell Sarah of the test of Isaac? (Genesis 22) We're not told. Sarah may have died not knowing about that test of faith. Or her heart may have been breaking with the knowledge while her husband and son were on the trip to Mount Moriah.

How heavy Abraham's heart must have been on the journey to sacrifice his promised son! How brutal that life test must have been for that family! How many of us could handle something like that? Yet Abraham trusted God. He proved worthy of that trust when God provided a lamb as an alternative offering. What a magnificent execution of devotion to God and following His command, despite its burden and great pain.

The true disciples, who walked closely with the Lord, discussed the cost of following Christ. Jesus never said it would be easy, laid back, just an interesting or even fun time. By contrast, He told them to anticipate the cost. In the KJV, Luke 9:23–24 says, "And he said to them all, 'If any man will come after me, let him deny himself, and take up his cross daily, and follow me. For whosoever will save his life shall lose it: but whosoever will lose his life for my sake, the same shall save it.'"

Jesus didn't pay people or bribe them to follow Him, or even intimidate them to abandon their current way of living. The disciples were at the point in their lives where they had to make a choice: Him or the world. I look at society today and it's amazing to see what we worship, place in the highest regard, pay rapt attention to, and on what we spend so much of our time: celebrities, world leaders, royalty, the wealthy, those who are self-absorbed in social and family networks, and others who steal our focus so much it takes our eyes off of Christ. Instead of worshiping the Creator, we too often worship His creations.

This book is about an important segment of my life. At first, it describes ordinary details that most people can identify with, but it soon develops into a nightmare I wasn't prepared for and had to be rescued from. I can only thank God for finally placing my kids and me into an environment I call a godsend. We still had to work hard to find ourselves and create a future with safety, purpose, and integrity, but our efforts were not being sabotaged daily. It was a refreshing change to live in a positive environment!

This story takes place when I was in my late twenties. I thought I knew the Lord and always loved Him, but the truth of the matter is, I didn't truly know Him. My early walk with Christ was all about my needs and wants, but there was never a time when I totally surrendered my life completely to Him. In a lot of churches today we're not trained to give our lives to the Lord completely. My walk for years was very shallow, looking out for old number one—me. "I need this done," or, "Please help with this or that." The truth is, I never gave much thought to how I might serve Him. It was all about me, and my needs.

Christ said, "If any... hate not... his own life... he cannot be my disciple," (Luke 14:26 KJV). And Paul said in 1 Corinthians 15:31 (KJV), "I die daily." Why? Because my human outlook—my "in look" perhaps—looked to me and my needs. But Christ commands us to come out of ourselves and become servants of Him. When you think about the judgment seat of Christ, and those who expect to hear, "Well done, my good and faithful servant," it's a mistake to think that anyone who never used their lives for Christ will ever hear those words from our Lord.

Every day we need to get up and say to ourselves, "Lord, help me put your desires before my own, so that you can live in me today, looking and seeing others as you do." This practice is the most important one on the planet. My heartfelt request is, "Help us, Lord, to lose sight of ourselves so that you can live freely through us."

Are we willing to do whatever it takes to be one of his disciples? Or are we like the man who came to the Lord in Matthew 19:16–22?
And behold, one came and said unto him, "Good Master, what good thing shall I do, that I may have eternal life?"

And he said unto him, "Why callest thou me good? There is none good but one, that is, God: but if thou wilt enter into life, keep the commandments."

The young man saith unto him, "All these things have I kept from my youth up: what lack I yet?"

Jesus said unto him, "If thou wilt be perfect, go and sell that thou hast, and give to the poor, and thou shalt have treasure in heaven: and come and follow me."

But when the young man heard that saying, he went away sorrowful: for he had great possessions. (Matthew 19:16–22 KJV).

Anointed Christians I know have paid a price for their sanctification by the Holy Spirit. And this hasn't changed in the twenty-first century. Some are criticized or avoided if their faith appears to set them apart, even if they're quiet and unobtrusive. Some fear offending others, if their faith is evident, and may be tempted to dilute His message, to avoid making others uncomfortable. Yet Jesus said, "And blessed is he, whosoever shall not be offended in me" (Matthew. 11:6 KJV).

I may have offended or puzzled others: associates at work, acquaintances, neighbors, distant family, even my husband. But as events evolved, my choice to live increasingly by resolute faith, replacing a more trivial faith, led me through trying times and the disappointing performance of social supports, those who seemed oblivious to the realities of my life or were aware but lacked empathy. Those two human traits may be opposite sides of the same coin, as awareness and empathy often can't be separated. Jesus said in Luke

10:2 (KJV), "Therefore, said he unto them, 'The harvest truly is great, but the laborers are few: pray ye therefore the Lord of the harvest, that he would send forth laborers into his harvest.'" (KJV). Meaning, some don't see the fields and harvest and willingly work in them, because they're too invested in self to work for another and receive the blessings of that devotion to our Savior.

The Lord had to take me to the end of myself so I could come into His presence. Yet Scripture plainly states, "No flesh will glory [boasting about oneself] in his presence … He that glorieth, let him glory in the Lord." (1 Corinthians. 1:29, 31 KJV)

Thus, even though I have experienced the divine, my faith preceding it was earnest, yet ordinary, with no right to feel special or superior. I was just incredibly blessed at a time when I was impoverished, and grateful for an increasing understanding of what our Lord expects from us, and will deliver to us. In the King James Version, John 20:29 says, "Jesus saith unto him, 'Thomas, because thou hast seen me, thou hast believed: blessed are they that have not seen, and yet have believed.'"

I hope you're challenged at the end of this book to ask, "Am I giving Him my all?"

This story is one of great anguish that my children and I endured due to a painful and verbally abusive marriage. We lived through it only by God's deliverance. The suffering my children and I went through still echoes in our minds to this very day. I still struggle with symptoms of post-traumatic stress disorder (or maybe it's not a disorder, but a natural and normal lingering, protective response to unreasonable conditions). My daughter has had panic attacks at times, and my son has issues as well, and may have for the rest of his life.

Although I'm thankful for the Lord's hand in my life, I'm sad for the unnecessary neglect we suffered.

I would like to invite you to become aware of people God has placed in your life that may need your help. It might be someone like I used to be—a struggling single parent who needs financial and emotional support but hates to ask for assistance. Look around, you might find your calling.

The Early Years

I was born in Illinois, into a middle-class family. My dad worked as a lithographer (printer) while I was growing up. Dad and Mom were both from a very small town in Tennessee, and they eloped when Mom dropped out of school at sixteen. She later got her GED, and Dad got a job in printing in Chicago. He was in a union, so he was a good provider.

Dad's origins: His mom, my grandmother, had dropped out of school in the third grade due to her mother's death, so she helped rear the younger kids on their small farm. She was such a diligent worker, planting the vegetable and flower gardens, canning the produce every autumn, and feeding the chickens, which provided eggs and meat. She also had to walk a mile to catch a ride with a friend in town who took her to work in a jeans factory. She never had a driver's license. But Grandmother did everything, including making all the kids' clothing. My dad always sang her praises.

Dad never mentioned his father much for whatever reasons which I may never know. My dad had four siblings, one an older brother who served in the Korean War and was never the same afterward. He sometimes stood outside in freezing weather, sweating profusely, perhaps from PTSD (called "shell shock" back then), but he wasn't officially diagnosed until 1980). Mom's origins: My mom's mom also worked in a local factory sewing jeans, and her husband's mom, my great-grandmother, lived with them, after having been married four times. My mom's dad drove a sand truck for construction sites, and they lived in a two-bedroom home with four children and the great- grandmother. That's a lot of people in a small house, but it had an enclosed porch in the back and some of the family slept there. Mom said they had homemade biscuits every morning and cornbread every evening; plus, they had great things from the garden. They raised chickens and pigs and had a smokehouse to preserve the meat. The only memory I have of my mom's dad was his love of buttermilk and cornbread, which he combined like a breakfast cereal. His personality was rather aloof, without any displays of affection, according to my uncle, my grandfather's only son.

My main memories though were of my two grandmothers, who were very attentive and loving; their husbands were less memorable and died while I was very young. We lived in Illinois, and they were in Tennessee, but we went back to visit at least once a year. We would visit one grandmother, then take her to visit with the other side of the family. That way the two women got the rare chance to see each other. Local transportation there wasn't well developed.

In this rural environment, formal education was not emphasized, local schools probably had few resources and life was just surviving. Awareness of the greater outside world, and any opportunities or advantages it might have, wasn't great. Even the older folks were limited in their knowledge of things distant, and monetary resources were very limited. Exploring other counties or regions, for opportunity or recreation, never occurred.

On the other hand, there was a kind of beauty to the simplicity of the rural lifestyle, the smiling faces of good neighbors, and the self-reliance that was learned at a very early age. The local schools closed for a few weeks when the cotton fields were being harvested, as everyone was expected to get this job done.

Kids grew up faster, in some ways, from these life experiences and responsibilities that many kids (especially now) never experience, which alters their mindset even as adults. So my mom marrying at sixteen wasn't uncommon back then, another facet of just surviving. Even though they eloped, they had gotten permission to marry from her parents, but were told they had to come back for a few days before going on to their first home—a small trailer in Blue Island, Illinois.

Even in my earliest memories, my parents always took us to church. I'm so thankful for that today. There were various services, the youth ministry, Awana, which focused on Bible awareness and committing some passages to memory, and quite a few other activities there. It seemed every time the church doors were open, we were there. Even with heavy Midwest blizzards, we almost always made it, no matter what, even though the church wasn't close by. We had devotional time some nights at home as well.

I remember my dad, the printer, making dollar bills with our pastor's face and name on them. Every Sunday, any child who attended would get such a dollar bill. We had a church store where they could pick out a prize with the number of "dollars" they had. My dad was the treasurer there as well, so he would count the real money after the services. These are amazing memories for me, of places and times and persons so special, never to be forgotten.

Grade school was pleasant for me, although my second-grade teacher frightened me because, as discipline, she sometimes would lift a child off the floor by their hair. I had long hair at the time, so you can imagine that I was one of her favorite best-behaved students. I was in Brownie Scouts, and I had a stay-at-home mom during those years. Mom had decided never to work outside the home again after my brother, when he was a toddler, reached for the percolator and was scalded with very hot coffee. He was in the hospital for months.

Mom blamed herself for allowing another family member to watch him, feeling it wouldn't have happened if she'd only been home.

Mom ran a tidy household, and meals were always on time. Bedtime was strictly enforced. Her organizational skills were impressive. She read herself to sleep with Harlequin romance novels while my dad worked nights. Mom was quite the peacemaker, having grown up in a house of turmoil, where screaming wasn't uncommon, especially whenever folks were together on weekends. I don't know if this also happened in my dad's family, but it seems like he never learned how to express frustration without raising his voice. So this happened often, and my mom just accepted it, not wanting to participate in a verbal fight. This may have been the origin of my avoidance of conflict, for sure with my dad, but sometimes with others, even if things were unfair. This also may have been part of my evolution as a people pleaser, which, of course, has some good attributes, but some vulnerability to being manipulated as well. I've had to work on this all my life, even in the present, because it's such an ingrained behavior, and gentle people can fear upsetting others who are perhaps more aggressive. But even people pleasers have their limits, needing justice and fairness in their lives, so flashes of anger can emanate from them as well. Dealing with anger, mine or someone else's, and controlling and processing it, instead of just flying off and saying things to regret later, is something I'll probably be working on until I draw my last breath.

Although my dad has wonderful attributes, the difficulty of handling frustration without anger is something I hoped I wouldn't pass on. But as an adult, I've had to apologize for going off on my own children. At least I recognized it as a problem, needing to learn to properly process stress and things going wrong, but it's still a weakness today that the Lord is helping me with. Change often happens slowly, even with earnest efforts to hasten the process.

My dad and his brother were close, so they decided to start a company in Pennsylvania, and we bought a home there, planning to move. They also bought a large warehouse that was about a city block long and transformed it into a folding carton plant. My dad did this while working his lithographer job on weekdays. I remember my uncle calling my dad frequently and us making trips in our camper and setting up camp inside the plant. My uncle had walked closely with the Lord at one time and even had thought he was called to preach, but sin got in the way, so he drifted away from God. But I loved him, and I know my dad did too.

My uncle was killed one night on an icy road when he lost control of his vehicle and hit a telephone pole. Seat belts were not always used in cars or trucks back then, so hitting a stationary object was often fatal. My dad had to fly out and bring his body back and sell off the company, even though it had shown such potential. I know all that must have haunted Dad. Mom told me he didn't sleep well for three years. I'm sure he still thinks of my uncle from time to time, a very good man, and also of their joy in working together on such a promising project. That was a difficult time for our family.

We ended up selling the home in Pennsylvania, and Dad got out of that business. Because of high home taxes in Illinois, and our wanting more land, we moved to northwest Indiana, where I started middle school, and my mother began cosmetology school.

My dad had a bit of a commute as he still worked at the same company location in Chicago. My brother and I asked to attend a Christian school because of kids we knew from church, so from then until graduation, we did so. I know things were tight, but my parents made a way. My dad worked on the church buses on Saturdays, and we went door to door, passing out brochures for the church and the gospel. My mom eventually owned her own salon, and since Saturdays are big in the hair industry, she was very busy those days. Passing out church brochures on Saturdays kept us busy as well, but no longer on foot. A friend, Dan, and a brother of mine used to drive us around to hand out brochures, and Dan was so funny. Every weekend when we got together, we took turns kicking a new dent in his car, just for the heck of it. And we laughed until there were tears—it was a junker, as you can imagine. Those are very fond memories.

My relationship with Christ was very vague, however. Not an intimately personal one, just a tradition—smile when needed, be responsible, and, of course, sing songs of worship. But there was no real application to my daily life. No one expected more, or perhaps no one understood what more might be conveyed in the New Testament about it, but our intentions were good. And as adolescents, we may have been protected by church, family, faith, and everyone looking out for each other.

When my brother was in high school, he suffered a motorcycle accident, riding on trails behind the house. He collided with a tree and sustained a very serious head injury. The ambulance was at our house when I got home from cheerleading practice. That was a pretty tough time. He was in a coma for five days, and it took years for him to recover. When he came home, he was very unclear about what was going on. I remember him putting toothpaste on his acne thinking it was Clearasil. One blessing though was that the hospital charges didn't demolish us, as Dad was in a union and had very good insurance.

My brother had played football in earlier years, and I was a cheerleader for one year. My first job was at Azar's Big Boy while in school. At age sixteen, I was training waitresses. Our school was very strict (for which I remain thankful). When I look at kids today and their immodesty and attempts to gain attention by wearing very little, it makes me sad. We didn't wear uniforms, but we had dress code checks—girls' skirts below the knee and the boys had hair checks (off the collar and ears).

My brother and I attended a Christian college. I had wanted to go to cosmetology school, but my parents told me there was no money in it, which was a little difficult for me to accept since my mom seemed to make good money from her shop. But there were so many issues I didn't feel I had permission to question my parents or an older sibling about, so I often just stored questions in my mind.

My parents were willing to pay for my continuing college, but I had no real direction at that time. I eventually attended cosmetology school, but not until many years later at age thirty-seven. It's hard to do well at school when you don't know what you want to do in the future. So I only went to college for one year. I didn't want to waste my parents' money, and no other skills or options were discussed at that time.

Again, in that era, in some families at least, openly discussing needs or wants or anything else without worrying about making someone else uncomfortable just didn't happen. Later, TV programs about family life probably made these things more accepted, and Americans now feel freer to allow practical family communication. I do wish I'd had a little more direction in what my options were, what careers were available without a college degree, and how I could get training for what looked desirable.

As a result, we really struggled when I became a single mom. What worked for one generation, such as that of my parents, may not suffice in the next, and not acquiring sufficient skills and certifications or degrees early on can certainly have unpleasant consequences. My dad had a good career and was in a union, and once told me, "I was in the best generation, where I could work for years in just one company and retire with really good benefits." I went to college for one year, and when coming home for my birthday that year, I met my future husband.

Life Changes: Meeting Richard

I met my husband while on a bus in Indiana. I was coming home from Tennessee for a birthday visit. We began a lively conversation on that Greyhound. I soon met his grandparents, who lived in a small town not far from where I was going to college. I loved going to their home; it was a little messy, but we would drink good coffee and his grandfather made us the best meals on his homemade brick grill. It was a nice experience, and I'm grateful I got to know both of his grandparents. They were both so charming with their welcoming spirit. Yet Richard and I were around each other only a short while before he left for basic training in the US Army. Then we communicated by letter and phone. I was waitressing and going to school.

My brother and I decided to share an apartment so I could save some money. Although only occasionally, I used to take Richard's grandmother out to lunch in fancy restaurants in Chattanooga, quite a distance away. Her husband stayed home, thinking a trek to a noisy metropolis was not appealing. He was such a homebody that he seemed almost planted at home. The roads up and over rural mountains in Tennessee were so curvy and steep that I'm surprised I never had much fear of driving them. But Richard's grandparents became like family, so while Richard was still around, he and I fished with his grandfather and just enjoyed nature and listened to stories of the old times.

Richard's stepdad was a weekend alcoholic, going up to Michigan to fish and get drunk by himself in his house trailer. He didn't even make it to Richard's high school graduation. His mom went from marriage to Richard's dad, a full-time abusive alcoholic, with five kids, to a marriage to a part-time alcoholic, who gave her three more kids to take care of, mostly on her own. Yet he never abused Richard's mom and was responsible in many ways.

The second husband's ex-wife had become a cocaine addict, incapable of caring for the kids, only taking care of her drug habit. How does a woman like Richard's mom take care of so many with so little? And how commonplace is this level of unfairness in the world at large? My parents really didn't care for Richard very much. I think they thought we were too different, but at first, they didn't really give me any details about their perceptions. I found Richard to be different from the men I'd known in my past. He was independent and had distinct opinions, but also was rather laid back, which appealed to me. But at some point, Dad did let me know that Richard seemed a little too opinionated at times and warned me that this kind of negativity might become a problem in the future.

Richard never coerced me in any way back then, and his criticisms of others didn't feel threatening to me, just someone else's transient observations. But I viewed him with a rather inexperienced set of perceptions, and my parents seemed to see things I didn't. When Richard first met my parents, my mom had tears in her eyes but said little.

There was little calm, open, calm communication in my family of origin, so questions about important personal choices didn't get processed effectively. I hope that occurs less today because families need to be able to communicate honestly, without fear of being made uncomfortable, simply needing to benefit from others' knowledge, thoughts, and feelings, and allow a healthy exchange of ideas.

Richard and I continued to date, but long-distance only. After my year of college, I came home to live with my parents to save money and worked as a photographer at a large store. Pretty soon Richard and I got engaged, then married. The night before the wedding, we went over to meet Richard's biological dad. He lived in a single-wide trailer on a farm he managed. Lots of crumpled newspapers littered the small enclosure. We visited for a while and then invited him to the wedding. Apparently, Richard had been too embarrassed to introduce us earlier as his dad had been a raging alcoholic, although he had stopped drinking by then. By raging, I'm not only talking about his serious alcohol abuse, but he also displayed a frightening anger to his family. It was so bad that his wife hid the children away during his worst tirades.

Richard's mom was sweet and passive, and ill-equipped to deal with the demons in her life. Those experiences, while detrimental in many ways, can sometimes confer protection too in the next generation. So while Richard had no reasonable male role models, he had been able to conclude that certain behaviors were without justification, and were not to be copied in his own life.

We had a lovely wedding at the church we were attending at the time, thanks to my mom and dad, and it was crowded. We also had a lovely wedding dinner catered, and I'm still thankful to my parents for that today. We honeymooned in a log cabin in Nashville, which I had to pay for because Richard hadn't been tracking his expenses. Hmmm.

We then went back to Richard's mom's house to get his things. That's when he informed me that he only had $200. His sister was a banker and oversaw his account and had told him what his balance was on the day of the wedding. We also used my car, as he no longer had one at the time. Hmmm. That was my second disappointment.

Being so in love, I just threw those thoughts under the rug. I wish I had taken more mental notes earlier on responsibilities.

The first few years of our marriage were good, nonetheless. We moved to Texas, where he was stationed at Ft. Hood, and we rented a home in the Killeen area. I fixed up the house and got a job at Olan Mills Studios selling portraits. I also sold additional pictures to families who had originally come in for just one or two. Richard was stationed there for eight months, and I really liked my job. Then he got transferred to South Korea, very close to the DMZ on the border with North Korea.

I stayed in Killeen and got a good job with a marketing company. Six months later, I had saved enough money to join Richard in Korea. That assignment was a nice experience. The way of life was very different from the States. I experienced new foods, shopping in small markets, getting custom made clothing, and just watching a very different culture. I look back now and recall that I used to jog through parts of town I didn't know —not the wisest thing to do. I couldn't believe the way mothers pushed young girls in front of soldiers in the open marketplaces, saying, "GI, want a girl?" I cringe thinking of that today, mothers prostituting their own daughters. (That kind of tragedy—sex trafficking—is still occurring today, and maybe even on a larger scale).

I did make friends at the USO by Camp Casey. I would take our clothing to the base and do the laundry; it was a far hike, but I didn't mind. I ate lunch a lot at the USO as it was American food; its familiarity was rather comforting. Richard didn't like the military, however, especially field assignments lasting several weeks at a time, with little time of his own. He decided he wanted to get out after his three- year enlistment was done. After serving his term, we went back to Indiana, which was a territory familiar to both of us. We initially rented an apartment my parents owned and looked for some opportunities.

My parents started an auction on Friday and Saturday nights, as an extra enterprise, so Dad offered both of us jobs. We helped organize the merchandise through the week when Dad was at his regular job, and Richard and I both worked Friday and Saturday nights at the scheduled auctions. I also enjoyed working in the concession stand. If someone tried to underbid an item, I lifted a number, on Dad's signal, which influenced other people to consider adding bids on that item. I chuckle when I think of that today. We had set prices on some merchandise if it were something Dad had a lot of money in, but everything else was sold on the bidding game.

I had fun setting up the auction like a store. My folks would drive to another state and pick up tractor-trailer loads of items from store liquidations and bring them back. The only downside was they couldn't pick out what was going into the truck. One time, a company filled it with virtually all handicapped items. These were things that a nursing home might have needed, but regulations prohibited anyone from buying any of these brand-new items from us. Instead, they had to order handicapped items directly from a supply company themselves.

A lot of the electrical things needed testing or refurbishing, so we had a guy who did that. My mom did the paperwork at the auction with her good friend and fellow cosmetologist. We had fun, and I certainly got the first choice on the merchandise. It turned out to be good training for future years in retail.

The Slippery Slope

Richard got a job at a local maintenance company. I began working in a women's clothing store. After two years of marriage, I became pregnant with our first child. Early on, I battled morning sickness carrying my daughter. It was rough. I remember going out to eat and losing it all over the table. Now and then, I had to lie down in the break room downstairs at work because I was feeling so sick.

As the manager of a store at an outdoor mall, I often had to close at the end of the business day. Several times Richard didn't pick me up after work, even when I had deposits to run to the bank at night, often in the cold of winter. I then had to call one of his family members to take me home. Carrying bags of money in a bad part of town wasn't only dangerous for me, but it also inconvenienced me and his family. The odd thing was that this recurring failure was the elephant in the room that no one talked about. It happened again and again and always involved alcohol, yet early on, I didn't see this as an ongoing problem. He constantly assured me it wouldn't happen again. We didn't have Uber or Lyft at that time, so I had to either call a cab or a family member. Even with the many rides home with one of his family, we never talked about why I needed the ride. Whether his family ever discussed it with Richard, I don't know, but that probably didn't occur either.

Three months into the pregnancy I remember waking up and realizing my husband hadn't come home from work at all that night. I quickly got dressed and rushed to where he worked only to find that they hadn't seen him since his last shift.

Richard showed up the next morning, thirty-six hours late and drunk, having driven himself home in that condition. I remember thinking, I can't tell anyone. So to protect him and us, I hid it. Our time together had been acceptably trouble-free up to this disconcerting event. What a mess! It felt so threatening to our security and tranquility. That was the first of too many such nights to come, worse than just not being on time to pick me up.

Had I possessed high self-worth at the time, I would have at least brought a counselor into the picture and insisted that Richard make it to the counseling appointments. Many men feel threatened by such interventions and refuse to be involved. He needed help I couldn't offer, but I didn't search for a counselor, for us or just me, because I felt that was too much to want. Instead, I tolerated the pain and uncertainty.

I've heard stories from my kids today, as told to them by their dad, which helps me understand some of the demons he battled and the scars he carried from having such an irresponsible and physically and mentally abusive biological father.

The Birth of Our Firstborn

After the birth of our daughter, Beth, I didn't think Richard would do anything to disrupt our lives further. But once or twice a year, Richard stayed out all night drinking and who knows what else. What an emotional prison that puts a spouse in! Just waiting a few minutes for his arrival caused me great worry regularly, never knowing whether it might be happening again. I would watch out a window with tears running down my face, wondering if he was coming home that night. My stomach was tied in knots, and sometimes I felt I couldn't catch my breath. It wasn't like he simply wanted to go out for a drink now and then and invited me to go with him. It was just a selfish impulse to abandon primary responsibilities and go straight from work to a bar, knowing that was unlikely to mean only one beer before going home to his young family eager to greet him, enjoy supper together, and the good feelings that were so available. He clearly wasn't motivated by needing to avoid an unpleasant home life.

My daughter was so amazing! She was eight pounds and thirteen ounces. I remember holding her in the hospital and thinking, I'll always be there for you. But by then, I had begun to realize I was in a terrible marriage. I didn't want to rear my precious daughter in that environment if I could help it. Richard was, nonetheless, very loving to his daughter, although still unreliable in the marriage.

The day I got home from the hospital with our newborn daughter, I received a call from a woman who told me she'd been with Richard in an intimate way. She said she was sorry and hadn't known he was married, or that I was pregnant, things she found out later.

For whatever reason, I never brought this terrible hurt to Richard's attention, or anyone else's. I never dealt with it. I didn't even know how to deal with it, so my way of coping with it was denial and devoting myself to my other family roles. Richard never mentioned this episode, although it damaged our relationship, and diminished my respect for my husband and myself even further. I was just too inexperienced to know how to deal with it directly. I didn't know I had options in such a dilemma, and I certainly didn't have an adequate support system where I could vent my disillusionment and sorrow. I probably feared telling anyone lest it generate gossip at work or in the neighborhood. I felt that it would only allow people to be judgmental, but not helpful. I've found that so many people can be like that.

Our home was full of folks dropping by to see our little angel. I find it strange today that I never addressed this affair with anyone.

After all, now I had a daughter to give my time and attention to, although that didn't heal the hurt from the adultery. I guess I kept it confidential to avoid embarrassment and small-town gossip or to pretend diligently that we were somehow okay and things would work out. That certainly was still my hope.

One night there was a snowstorm, and I thought Richard hadn't come home, until I looked outside the next morning, and saw him asleep and, drunk, in his car. So I ran out and hustled him into the house so the neighbors wouldn't see him. The anxiety of my husband not returning home during bad weather, with no phone call, and then having to get him out of his car into the house was hurtful and frustrating. And then he never apologized for his ridiculous behavior. Maybe he had learned as a child that the women in his family just kept working and working and taking care of almost everything, no matter how AWOL the man in the family was.

Home life with Richard was a mixed picture, to be sure. One time, I hosted a dinner for another couple we knew. At one point during the evening, I tried to give Richard a kiss. For whatever reason (never explained), he quickly turned away. I never initiated public affection with him again, of any kind, having been treated so rudely. However, we never discussed it as many things in my family of origin hadn't made me feel safe enough to bring up, to clarify, and to learn from. If in doubt, silence was the safer alternative, which I had learned while growing up.

All household chores were done by me, which in the late 1980s and early 1990s was no longer the rule in most all-American marriages. This too was never discussed. In my original family, the same pattern existed to some extent, although the culture at that time was supportive, as many women didn't work outside the home. Although I do recall that my dad helped around the house. I stayed home after the birth of each child, about fifteen months each, before returning to work. While working, I also had most of the evening childcare and home chores to do, which pattern, unfortunately, seems to continue even now in many homes. Progress often seems to happen but seems may be the key word. How many men do you know who clean the bathrooms in their homes? Mowing the lawn is a manly chore and nice and clean, but bathrooms seem to get maintained by someone else. Too many germs lurking, I guess.

In retrospect, Richard had displayed so many ways of controlling people around him. I had just never noticed it in the early years. Over time, this manifested itself in his constant criticism of others, including me. That was so exhausting that I simply stopped responding rather than start an argument.

Richard had a very cold side to him, not evident early in our relationship. Perhaps this was a latent trait he picked up in dealing with his challenging family of origin, or possibly a compensation for his inability to discipline the processes in his troubled mind. He seemed to be changing over time, and not for the better.

I still had notions that I needed to be the steadfast, stable, patient force that held our family together. This wasn't the result of a single decision by me, just an expression of my personality and values. But over time, the mostly fair, mutual support became frayed, and not from anything in evidence from our earlier, successful years together. This was something new, unnamed except for incidents and attitudes, and as such, unidentified, and not anything my experience had prepared me for, even though it was starting to resemble some past family history.

Besides puzzlement about what was happening, I felt lonely—lonely in my own home. An increasing number of things couldn't be discussed without potentially evoking an argument, and the sweet little nothings, supportive or affectionate expressions, had mostly vanished from our home life. I no longer felt respected, certainly not loved, and that isolated me emotionally and produced a feeling of loneliness, even in the company of my spouse.

In those days, sometimes even now, the average person may know little about mental illness. It's rarely taught or discussed in public schools or even in required college courses. How to write an essay may be required, for good reasons, but something about recognizing and dealing with maladaptive behavior might be even more useful.

I continued to make excuses, covering for his behavior to all who knew us. In those days, there often were no therapists in small towns, no social workers, psychologists, or psychiatrists, with only local ministers or friends trying to assist the afflicted. And they often lacked the capacity, competence, or willingness to try to help out a couple in distress.

Even to this day, men (not just Americans) continue to resist entering marital or family therapy, preferring to pretend that that would be an unwanted acknowledgment of failure. Or they fear that some of their domestic authority or proud independence could become compromised. Some even rationalize this irresponsibility with biblical quotations from patriarchal sections of the Old Testament, reflecting an ancient culture where men were simply expected to dominate women. This leaves millions of families of all kinds without needed assistance, which, if available, could save so much heartache, including emotional (even physical) trauma to the children in these homes.

But there were also good things happening. As a baby, my daughter loved the swing. While I cooked, she sat and watched—, my little kitchen buddy, and such a special one at that. She cried when the swing stopped but became calm after I wound it up again. I was so fortunate with her. Once she was asleep, I could take her anywhere and she wouldn't wake up. Her nursery was a Mickey and Minnie Mouse theme. We'd been hard-pressed to get the nursery done before her birth. But I knew this one thing: I loved being a mom!

While staying home and taking care of my daughter, I earned money by watching another toddler. I also did accounting for a businessman in our church. His office was so close I could walk there to update the books and write out payroll checks. So by this time, my social isolation was well underway, the downside of not being out in the world. It's funny looking back now, to realize that I felt I couldn't talk about the growing marital problems when I should have sought help without shame. But shame is something that develops in these dysfunctional relationships when who is to blame has become puzzling. Even a manipulated and innocent party begins to take on this toxicity, because, like so many other women, I found my identity in my husband. So independent assessment of me couldn't just happen, with my level of experience, and yet my need to keep on trying continued.

After two years of living in an apartment, we bought a small home in Indiana, with his VA loan, no money down. The house was eighty-four years old, built with a Sears Roebuck kit, and with horsehair plaster walls! We replaced it with modern drywall and tried to make it into a desirable living space. We put in another bathroom upstairs, and French doors opening from a bedroom to a large second-floor deck we also added on. The home was beautiful and inviting by the time we finished. This had a reassuring effect on me: things going in a good direction, and a wonderful home for our young family.

The work on the house took a long time, even with a little help from several relatives, including Richard's biological dad. At one point, I heard him say, "I've had the pleasure of living my own life." My immediate thought was, How sick. You brought four people onto the planet and had no regard for their well-being.

Richard's biological dad was indeed a strange person, had been a terrible alcoholic years ago, but had mostly sobered up. He used to beat the other children when he came home in a rage but spared his eldest son (my husband) for some reason, perhaps because Richard was his firstborn son, and that helped his dad identify with him. He did help us refurbish the Indiana house since he knew how to replace drywall, repair the old double-hung windows, and repair or replace dysfunctional plumbing. He was on good behavior except for occasional foul language, which I didn't appreciate in my daughter's presence, even though she was just a toddler at the time.

Richard's mom was very sweet, and she divorced his dad later in Richard's childhood. She then married a guy who just drank on weekends when he would go fishing on a river in Michigan. She was kind, almost too kind since she was unwilling to discipline Richard. I don't believe she set regular limits as she should have, but maybe she had so much going on she felt as though she couldn't. The second husband had three children and she had five herself, one an adopted cousin. I know life was very busy for them, certainly for her. She likely did her best to find a somewhat less-damaged second husband, although she probably had too little personal power to make truly big changes for herself and all the children in her care.

Trying to Understand

I didn't fear my husband when we were dating, nor early in our marriage, but once I was pregnant and more vulnerable, Richard began not coming home in the evening now and then, without telling me anything. My fears increased over time as the terrible combination of irresponsible and controlling behaviors developed. At times, I didn't feel it was worth it or even safe for me to object and try to reason with him. And that may be why I allowed myself to be put into the somewhat humiliating role of becoming a servant in my own home. Sitting at the supper table, Richard would snap commands at me, such as, "Get me some tea!" and stare at me (as an intimidation flourish) when it was within his reach. That behavior might have been common in the early 20th century, but not in the early 1990s. Yet I lived it daily at our house, which could hardly be called a home.

My nerves were constantly on edge. I was unprepared for this, was continuously stressed, and didn't know what was wrong with him, or with us. Not knowing why things are going wrong is an additional crazy maker. Was it me, as he implied? Or him, which seemed the reality in plain sight? Or was it us, just a bad combination? It would take me years to understand and overcome the damage from this turbulent relationship.

At one point, we got a new car for Richard to commute with. After only a few weeks, he put a bumper sticker on it, which said, "My wife said if I go fishing again, she's going to leave me. God, I'm going to miss her." Utterly disrespectful, yet he no doubt expected it to entertain coworkers neighbors, and anyone else in our small town, as if that were an acceptable value instead of a form of very public hostility. Not something as subtle as being passive-aggressive by simply not doing something I or we needed. An external expression of his problem with contempt. That sarcastic bumper sticker was never removed, and I don't recall ever complaining to him about it, lest I receive more criticism and selfish justification than I was already dealing with, almost daily. What wasn't present, were any thanks, faint praise, or apology for things. That really hurt.

My local support system was sparse. I wasn't working outside the home at this time and thus had no exposure to coworkers, who sometimes can become helpful to a person in distress. There was a nice couple a few houses down in the neighborhood, who seemed good prospects for friendship, but I was hesitant to visit them or invite them over, sensing disapproval from Richard. I was also afraid of the real possibility of my embarrassment if the couple spent an evening with us and Richard got into one of his critical or sarcastic moods. Thus, the home environment was chronically toxic and devoid of life-enhancing experiences, even a kind word or simple thanks. Yet I felt I couldn't improve things with some nice experiences with friends or neighbors, because there was so little consistent respect.

Richard had friends from work, and sometimes he helped them with errands or home improvement tasks after work. But he never phoned to let me know where he was and when he might be home. Supper was always ready on time, but on many occasions, the children and I ate alone. When Richard did come home, he often had alcohol on his breath. This pattern, unfortunately, presaged his later increase in drinking, sometimes with coworkers after their shift, and later, just going to bars where he knew no one.

Back then it became a cause of misery, unnecessary misery. Yet today in the United States, misery is still a common problem for families in trouble and for people living alone, whose basic emotional needs aren't being met. Social isolation of various kinds keeps the person stuck in this situation. So many people come up with various reasons for not networking socially, not taking chances on making new acquaintanceships that might evolve into friendships and meaningful interaction and mutual support with understanding, gentle advice, or simple empathy.

Just knowing that someone else knows can be the start of reaching out, which can evolve into a better perspective, and the opportunity to discuss what options the suffering party might have. Many constructive TV shows have, in recent decades, reduced the stigma of having personal problems. Yet old thinking patterns, and anxieties from childhood about what other people think, can nonetheless keep even an intelligent and experienced person from disclosing what's begging to come out, respectfully and constructively, not condemning one's partner or complaining just to complain. If you weren't reared in a family whose problem-solving skills extended to emotional issues and relationship building, then a marriage that evolves badly can seem confusing and soon overwhelming. The tools to repair it may not be known, and even seeking effective help can raise anxiety by its potential financial cost and the semi-public declaration that something is a little wrong or very wrong. Family therapy can be very effective when done well, but getting the whole system involved often doesn't happen, in many cases due to a reluctant male. Silence and suffering. Uncertainty about options. Innocent children become puzzled and feel troubled as well, not understanding why interactions at school seem mostly fair and interactions at home seem constantly tricky. Being meek and silent seems the safest option to them.

42

Under constant stress and criticism, there's a point in dysfunctional relationships where even a strong person begins to give up on anything but passive acceptance that this is life, and no clear exit is available. Divorce still had a stigma to it in the early 1990s, and even if you weren't concerned about it for yourself, there was concern about how it might be perceived by your family of origin, or townspeople in a small gossipy town, or even the friends and classmates of your children. I probably was too concerned about that, yet in constricted situations where there isn't a close dependable friend from whom to get perspective, possibly making more mistakes seems quite scary.

Even writing this book—such an important project for me—has caused me to re-experience some of the dread and worry that used to be a part of my everyday life. At times, I had to walk away from writing, just recalling the traumatic years sending me back into a tailspin. Looking at photos of myself during that time reminds me that it had been like I was in a shell— … just existing. And back then, I'm sure I said to myself, Well, I'll probably live another forty more years or so, but maybe I can get through this.

Why does this matter? This long chapter has been about daily misery and how it may not get resolved when it should… or ever. Because a life lived minute by minute, hour to hour, is all we have. We experience safety and satisfaction or even moments of joy, or learn to live without these things, and push forward with our quality of life that is so compromised, trying to get by, hoping for better, yet trapped by all the various factors I've described. This is our life. This is what matters. This hell on earth is a daily reality for too many, and I hope that what I lived for too many years can motivate you to discern others you know, who might be caught up in a situation they don't deserve, like I was. Or if this is your life to suffer, this will guide you in some way to seek help or introduce a rescue of sorts from the outside, from persons who know how to resolve these destructive and unnecessary things. If you don't know where to turn, consider praying for help from the Lord, like I did, knowing there is one who cares.

God is no respecter of persons. What He did for me, He can do for you as well!

Time for Change?

What never got even modestly corrected was Richard's unreliability—I never knew what a day would bring. One night Richard came home first and acted like he'd fallen asleep. He then snuck out while I was sleeping. I later found out that he had cashed his paycheck instead of bringing it home, and even bought rounds of drinks for strangers in a bar! The manager of the clothing store I worked at came in and told me she had seen my husband at a local bar.

I had finally had enough! I called my parents and drove over late in the night, crying, with my toddler daughter still in her sleeper. I shared all about his drinking, not being reliable, and sometimes not picking me up from work or not even coming home after work. And my parents listened. I thought, it's over now, but nothing changed, not even my family's discomfort or inability to discuss difficult topics. So any hoped-for new tradition of calmly assessing a situation and coming to some mutual conclusion was still missing in action. Too much to hope for.

I stayed a few nights with my parents before driving back home, knowing nothing was going to change with them, or for me. And I feared leaving Richard because I couldn't support us by myself. I believe this is why so many people stay: without proper skills, how do you get out and support not only yourself but also your children and childcare while you're at work? And if you haven't had the forethought to put away some escape money, that avenue doesn't exist. Even in 1990, the thought of divorce seemed less than fully acceptable to me. Yet that reality left me living in fear, day after day.

My parents didn't know what I could or should do, had no similar experiences themselves, and didn't know how to research this. Their circle of friends might not have had helpful advice if the information had been shared. There was no Internet or Google to look up options available. And even back in the 1990s, more so before that, people didn't freely inquire of others about very personal things, especially small-town folks, who might be concerned about the risk of local gossip (defined as judgmental persons who become aware of domestic disaster but offer no help and make others afraid to seek help from their friends and neighbors).

One thing I tell young ladies today is to get a life skill or college degree or certification. Set yourself up financially, and never lose your identity in a relationship, especially before you've lived on your own. Your best friend can be your growing identity and capability. Living on one's own, either in school or with a job, with or without a roommate, as a learning transition between the family of origin and future family in marriage, is a profoundly important phase of life. Just ask someone who has never experienced it how they feel when their first marriage is in trouble, and they realize they never had a taste of independence and self-reliance and paying the bills all on their own.

Richard promised he wouldn't stay out all night drinking again. And he supposedly received Christ on three separate occasions, getting into the Bible for a while, with me hoping that this time maybe things would change. We needed that. But even when he was only ten minutes late coming home from work, I would start crying, thinking he wasn't going to arrive. If he did arrive in a few minutes, I hurriedly dried my eyes, put a smile on, and to spare him being embarrassed and needing to explain himself, pretend, yet again, that maybe something had delayed him (at a time when cell phones were a rarity). Even when he pretended to recommit to Christ, that lasted only a few days and later appeared just to be a manipulation.

We had enough challenges with impulsivity, lying, and no-shows without phone calls. Now the near-naked next-door neighbor was added into the mix. No wonder I was a bundle of nerves! She used to work for Hooters, and I sometimes noticed her walking around outside her house indecently dressed. I was already feeling insecure, both about myself and more about my husband and our relationship. I simply asked him not to go over there. Then I came home one day, and my daughter told me that Richard had been in the neighbor's house "fixing something." I was hurt, one more time, and it wasn't going to be of any help to try to reason with him or somehow obtain a new commitment from him.

I was a plastic person, not having and accepting thoughts of my own. Instead, I focused on how I could make this miserable marriage work, focused on Richard, unable to see myself objectively, and how I wasn't the origin of the problems. This self-blame wasn't appropriate but derived from inexperience. Not having stable thoughts of your own, and a secure identity, is indeed more likely if you've gone straight from living with your parents to living with a husband and depending on him. You have no experience of independent living to provide an identity or tools to withstand difficult times. Or, for that matter, create good times, with or without another person.

With my folks knowing I was in a bad marriage, and with me very aware of it as well, I found out I was pregnant again. I recall my mom advising me not to have any more after this one, as she knew that the future was clouded.

I had little morning sickness this time and less weight gain, so it was much easier than my first pregnancy. I hoped for a boy this time, and nine months later we did have a healthy son. He was a large baby at nine pounds and thirteen ounces. We named him Brad. What sweet, lovely children we had! My son received a pair of baby cowboy boots that he was never able to wear, just to give you an idea of his large size. He had blonde hair and blue eyes, just like me. He was so perfect! What a gift! And yet the context he was born into was so very troubled.

At first, when we got home from the hospital, Richard seemed so happy coming home at night and focusing on our family. I know I was thrilled to have my baby boy, but simultaneously, I didn't think Richard would turn out to be an acceptable role model in our son's future. I always told myself, if he gets a DUI, I'm out of here. But really, how could I leave, when I had no real source of income and a paralyzing fear of so many things? All the verbal abuse had taken effect. I had no idea who I was.

One day when I got home from work, Richard was holding Brad. He informed me he had just ordered a $1000 engine, despite neither of our cars needing an engine at that time. Then he proceeded to tell me that he was going to teach our son, then five months old, how to work on engines. We had not discussed this, so his purchase was both impulsive and totally impractical. There was no room in our tight little budget as it was, and he refused to cancel the order.

He occasionally said demeaning things when we were in public. He had mood issues, and in some states of mind, not influenced by alcohol, he would just stare at me or one of his children and state something hurtful, for no apparent reason. He did that to our son one day, who was in a happy mood and causing no trouble. His father just looked at him at close range, and said, "Wimp," not explaining that to his son or family. He often said hurtful things, then just acted like this was normal behavior.

Often when the family was having a good time, he would shout, "What are you all so happy about?" Since he had issues with his mood, he may have been envious of family members enjoying their good moods and healthy, open interactions. It's quite sad, frankly, to see someone needing to trash others to level the playing field. But this happened on countless occasions, with negative effects on the children and on our marriage, which ultimately, he didn't cherish and nurture.

Whatever he wanted, he bought. That was a real change from earlier years when there were no financial conflicts. Was he getting ill, or was he being influenced by drugs or something else I couldn't discern? When things change over a long period of time, we sometimes don't fully recognize them as major alterations, even alarming patterns, as they tend to become familiar over time, even if they're annoying or puzzling during that period. How can you understand what's going on with another family member when you know it's not a result of alcohol? Another drug? A slow-moving mental illness? All sorts of things run through your mind. And who has the training to figure that out? Not knowing just adds to the puzzlement, and the coming and going of disturbing behavior leaves you unable to predict what the next day will bring. Richard's controlling nature and constant criticism seemed to become habitual over time, instead of being intermittent and being such a daily irritation. For instance, he insisted that I wait on him at the supper table as if I were his waitress. He expected me to accommodate him in whatever he chose to do. I was still a people pleaser at the time so that eventually caused more morale problems for me. We continued to pretend we had a normal life, even though I was feeling increasingly demoralized and felt I was living a lie. I felt so unappreciated in the relationship.

I remember one time when we went on a family vacation with my parents and my brother's family, out on the ocean in Florida. I was playing in the water with the kids, and Richard just came up to me and said, "Aren't you ready to go?" How ridiculous it felt not to be allowed to have a restful and pleasant time.

Nonetheless, Richard got a really good job opportunity in maintenance with a big company, and we started looking for places where we could move. When we went to Tennessee to see where my parents had grown up., Richard decided he really liked the South. He soon found out that the company had a plant in Oklahoma, but also one in Georgia. We looked in Oklahoma first, but it wasn't a fit for us. So we went to Georgia and found nice brand-new homes for under one hundred thousand dollars on an acre of land, so we decided to buy there.

Things were looking up and seemed to be going pretty smoothly. I tried to stay hopeful. Richard began settling into his new job, and I was busy setting up our home just the way we wanted it. We did some painting and some landscaping. Soon our children settled into the new home. How I wanted the best for them!

But inside, I knew things could change at any minute. We didn't keep alcohol in the house, although Richard brought a little home on a few occasions. Things might have deteriorated more rapidly had we always kept a stock of liquor.

Then the bottom fell out again. I received a phone call late at night from the local police department. Richard had been arrested for a DUI. My nightmare had come true. This was not the life I wanted for myself or my children. I got up in the middle of the night and went to get him out of jail. One thing I'm not good with is geography, especially at night, and there was no GPS at the time, so it was a real struggle to navigate the town at night, pay the bail, and bring him home.

Even though I felt I needed to figure out how to disentangle myself from my daily hell, bringing up the topic of trying a separation for a while to Richard, or just getting a divorce, made me understandably nervous. Unfortunately, amicable discussions or negotiations were not a possibility with someone so defensive that he took any requests for possible change as an attack on his identity as the head of household who should be totally in charge.

On one occasion when I broached this possibility, he immediately began arguing with me and blaming me for all kinds of things. On his way out of the house, he disconnected the phone line outside and pulled something out of my car's engine compartment so it wouldn't start. He later took his name off the credit card that had the engine purchase on it, leaving me with a maxed-out card with a variety of other mostly unplanned, never-discussed items he had bought on impulse.

In my mind, I began planning an exit strategy.

A few months later, while Richard was at work, I had a realtor come out to our home to give me an evaluation. As I showed the realtor around, I started crying, trying to explain what was happening. He responded by quoting Romans 8:1 (KJV), "There is therefore now no condemnation to them which are in Christ Jesus, who walk not after the flesh, but after the Spirit." (KJV).

That was the first time I'd ever heard that passage. Such words of freedom. Not having much knowledge of the Holy Spirit at that time, I couldn't believe there was a way out in the Scripture. Whereby a well-intentioned person like me, long-suffering, might make a justifiable change, and have any guilt removed.

Divorce, Deliverance, and Freedom

After the realtor left, I went upstairs to my room and knelt by the bed. I cried out to the Lord, "I don't know how to get out of this, and I don't know if I even have the strength! Please help me, dear Jesus."

Sometime thereafter, I told Richard I wanted a divorce, and he started throwing me around the room. He traveled a lot for his job at the time and had just returned home. After a few minutes, I picked myself up, and went downstairs, and dialed 911. The police took Richard with them when they left.

The next day when I came home from work, I found myself locked out. I took the kids to our friends across the street. I remember sitting at my neighbors' home, having a glass of wine, and telling them all about our circumstances. I was trying to process things, thinking, this is finally happening. I stood and stared at my home across the street and knew it would never be the same again. Then I briefly went back over to the back of the house to see if Richard was home. I saw him through the window, working on installing the new locks. I called the police again from the neighbors' house, and they had him removed the next day.

Fortunately, at some point, Richard moved in with a godly, older friend, who had opened up his home to him. I contacted a cheap attorney to set up meetings and get the divorce proceeding started, as the one thing missing in my life was any sort of boundaries or structure. I was used to letting people walk all over me, and was always apologizing for things, a true sign of weakness. No, of great demoralization. A truly beat-up soul.

The next morning, I looked in the Yellow Pages of the phone book (we still used those in the nineties) and saw an ad for a Christian daycare. I knew I had to have childcare for my children in order to look for a full-time job, so I called and told Ms. Barbara, the director, what I'd been going through. She said that in the Old Testament the Lord had allowed divorce for the hardening of hearts. She had such a mild and reassuring voice. Unbeknownst to me, she would come to be a larger influence in my life than I could possibly have imagined. Ms. Barbara was often very direct in sharing her insightful observations when I was in her presence, but she did so in such a gentle manner that any perceived criticism wasn't hurtful. She was simply sharing her abundance of wisdom.

I brought the children in and, while looking throughout the daycare, I met Ms. Barbara and her lovely staff. She told me, "I prayed for you in intercessory prayer last night at church on the campus, and the Lord is delivering you: He wants you right here." So they placed my son in daycare and my daughter in kindergarten, and offered me a job and, hopefully, a place of great healing. There was a church and a school, kindergarten through high school, and the daycare, all on one campus. Everyone referred to each other by first names, like Ms. Barbara and so on. For the first time in a very long time, I was being shown respect. I remember how difficult it was to receive it.

The campus was very lovely, off the beaten path, and had a great sense of privacy. All the buildings were separate on twenty acres of grass with many mature trees. This became a sanctuary for my mind and body in a time of desperately needed healing. I'd lost a lot of weight and had trouble keeping my thoughts on track. Apparently, this was a result of always being distracted and stressed, wondering what Richard was saying or doing, and replaying all the lies and the cover-ups.

Getting my mind back in focus really took time and a reassuring stable environment. It was truly a growth experience for me, an experience I wouldn't trade for anything else. I was shown respect and consistent and pervasive dignity for the first time in my whole life. I spent a full three years working in this dramatically different environment, soaking up accurate positive information about myself, and about the one who inspired their impressive integrity. I began to heal and become confident again. I drew strength and identity from the Holy Spirit, who would never fail me.

I had a family home there, and for once, people weren't telling me to stay and work it out, which some Christian friends had done in the past. I began to become strong in myself. But I also realized the danger of placing my identity totally in another person. We must each have our own identities. But most of all, our identity must come from Christ. And Him alone.

Yet for people expecting detailed direction on how to address a bad marriage that can't seem to be worked out and put back on track, the Scripture doesn't provide clear guidance for that. Christ never provides detailed solutions, but this gray area needs to be discussed in our churches today. Christ did say, "Love your neighbor as you love yourself," and there is no closer neighbor than your spouse. Conflict doesn't necessarily change this, although if a relationship becomes destructive or dangerous, establishing emotional and physical distance may become very necessary. No one should argue against that.

For years I tried to speculate on what was wrong. It's just this one thing he does that's so irritating to me, or it's this other thing that's dangerous to our marriage. But that was just it; I was giving him all the power and not standing up for myself. The unequal power, and often uneven responsibility that was distorting the relationship and various parts of our lives, made life puzzling. It undermined my confidence, not only in him, but also in myself. And a regular diet of put-downs eventually erodes your identity and self-esteem and makes it hard to know if any particular criticism is valid. And an environment where you should expect positive reassuring comments, yet one is ever forthcoming, is another important factor that over time reduces confidence, erodes any intimacy or closeness of any kind, and creates low morale. Even mature, intelligent, emotionally stable people need (and deserve) daily reminders—little ones or big ones—that you're okay, that you're admirable, and most importantly, that you're lovable. Once a week or once a month might suffice during an unusual circumstance, but most of us need more frequent affirmations of our value.

Richard and I met for a joint attorney meeting at an office in Atlanta. I had a cheap attorney, and he had a lady from a high-end firm. Because I only had a job making minimum wage and Richard had a great job and a big-time attorney, I went to the meeting alone—not a good idea— and signed a contract stating that if I stayed in the house in Paulding County, it would be set up as a trust for the children. I wasn't sure that was the most needed agreement, but nonetheless, that was included in the divorce. Richard was to pay the mortgage, and I was responsible for everything else. Only much later did I realize that I was so beat down at the time, that I didn't know what to ask for or to insist on. I certainly had never been in a situation like this before.

I felt I was lucky to get the children for the school years and Richard got them weekends and summers. I had no way of proving he was unstable; one DUI is hardly grounds for losing custody. But the Lithia Center put positives and hope back into our daily life. I loved the staff. And the pastor's wife, Ms. Bunnie, also was there a lot. She and Ms. Barbara were strong Christ-like women, and a great comfort to me. Ms. Bunnie wore Red Door perfume, which instantly made me aware of her presence whenever she was in the building. I still sometimes smell that fragrance on purpose in a store when no one sees me using the counter sampling display. It's such a pleasant memory. Please don't think I'm a saint. My life had plenty of sin in it at the time, which I told Ms. Barbara one day. She gently placed her hand on my shoulder and replied, "We're only human." Ms. Barbara always had encouraging things to say.

She was the one who assured me that I was being delivered.

Ms. Barbara, Founder of the preschool

Our classroom

My children and I took photos on campus

Every morning while we drove the twenty minutes to daycare, I quoted Psalm 118:24 (KJV), "This is the day the Lord hath made: we will rejoice and be glad in it." (KJV). Then the children and I would talk about what we hoped for that day. Ms. Barbara had said, "It was prophesied by a visiting evangelist that this church center and its organizations were going to be a place of refuge." And it was for us. Driving up the hill to the campus, sometimes I wondered how my life's twists and turns came out like this. I also felt how fortunate we were to be with these lovely people and the unselfish help they gave.

I worked from 8:00 a.m. until 6:00 p.m., but the children were right there on the campus with me, and it was a place of great peace. I was placed in the baby room, and I could listen to gospel music while I worked. Sandi Patty's music was always an encouragement to my soul. What a voice! But I kept the music playing softly while I held and fed the precious children. I sometimes had times of sorrow and tears while the children were sleeping. And it gave me time to reflect on what had happened in my marriage.

Richard made the house payments, and I continued to pay the utilities, on my more limited income. It was amazing! The Lord always provided. And I did have food assistance from some church pantries. It's funny, after going through it myself, years later, I have my hand in a food ministry. At the childcare center, I had a chart hung on the door with magnets to tell each parent how much formula or food each child had eaten, how they had done at nap times, and other details of their day. This was the beginning of regaining order in my life again and realizing the importance of a schedule. I'm so thankful that I had people around me with great patience and understanding. I became friends with a lot of the moms of the children in the daycare center as well. There was a great sense of community, and I made nice friends who were kind and predictable and dependable, factors I had needed so much in my daily life. I sometimes got compliments, which I found I had a little trouble accepting.

I once asked Ms. Barbara, "Do you know how long it has taken me to recognize the truth again, and feel confident in it?"

She smiled and seemed to understand completely.

I attended church on the campus and grew so much in Christ. Of course, I don't think I really understood Him. Or how to know Him personally. Sometimes when I stood near Ms. Barbara, my knees trembled with the presence of the Holy Spirit. I once asked her, "What did you pay for the anointing of the Holy Spirit?"

She replied, "Everything."
Those words never left me.

Richard lived with an elderly Christian male friend, and what a wonderful person he was! He treated our children like gold. My adult daughter wants to name a child after him. I'm glad Richard had him as a friend. Even though Richard really hurt me, I didn't want bad things for my ex. We have to forgive those who trespass against us.

Melda was our cook at Lithia Christian Center. She always wore her hair in a bandana and wore long culottes and a baggy blouse. She was constantly bringing me special treats. I said to her on several occasions, "I don't know where I'd be without this organization."

She would just smile and say, "God is good, huh?" And reassure me about my future, "Wherever the Lord places you." Sadly, years after I was out of that ministry, Melda went home to be with the Lord after a bout with cancer.

I started to really work on my emotional healing. I still felt so much fear being around loved ones. I knew they loved me, but they were also quite overpowering with a touch of intimidation, or I worried they would withhold affection or approval. But the real damage to my body and soul occurred from a slowly accelerating bullying that had taken place over a ten-year relationship. Those were hard years, being married to an alcoholic, never knowing what the day or night might bring, always wondering, Will he come home tonight or stay out drinking? The emotional prison that places someone in is mind-blowing. I guess enough people know that today, and that's why we have Al- Anon as a support system for the alcoholic's family members.

I believe alcoholism is an illness, possibly a mental illness, certainly an ingrained vulnerability. Not being able to rely on someone's word is heartbreaking, especially when you're married to them. And that allows a pervasive uncertainty about any commitments or routines that you need to depend on. This uncertainty generates ongoing anxiety throughout each day and even at night, making falling asleep, staying asleep, and not having unpleasant dreams a new difficulty in your life. Being a single mom isn't easy! You try to be enough support for each child, while attempting to deal with the world each day. And working a full-time job while trying to build myself back up and watch out for the kids seemed to be a little much. After years of trying to deal with a chaotic and contentious marriage, instead of having a source of emotional comfort and daily stability, I was slowly healing myself emotionally while giving my children consistent support.

I still felt continually stressed during this time, haunted by the uncertainties, wondering when life might become less difficult and more predictable. My environment was so much more stable at the center and at home, and I now had a routine. Nonetheless, my body expressed some of my chronic distress by developing a swelling in my neck, which had no other explanation. But the improved environment was also helping my health in some noticeable ways. My low weight began returning to normal, because I could now relax when eating and didn't feel so vigilant all the time as when the marriage was hellacious. With the passage of time, and reading the Bible daily, I could feel myself getting stronger and stronger. And each evening, I asked the Lord for strength. Only He can really understand what a broken person feels like.

An example of recurring stress was when the children were away all summer with my ex. I still took care of everyone else's kids for three months, with tender loving care, but my mind kept returning to my own children. Some days it felt like I could just give up! Thank goodness for empathic support from others who cared, a good word here and there, a hug when really needed, and a safe working and living environment.

Any of us can strive to notice others, and sometimes their subtle signs of distress or discouragement, and ask the right question or make a supportive statement. At the same time, we can avoid being judgmental and negative. Like Mark Twain said many years ago, helping another out in a seemingly simple way is often very appreciated, and for the person doing so, just no problem (perhaps the origin of the popular expression, "No problem," after someone says, "Thanks").

Ms. Darcie worked next to me in the baby room. She was a little heavyset and always wore her hair in a bob haircut. She had worked at the center for many years and had had a hard childhood that she was still trying to overcome. She had a devoted husband and a daughter. But there was one thing we knew not to do, which was to take anything out of Darcie's room, or there would be a price to pay. Everything was labeled, "Darcie." That suggests she may have had a childhood where possessions and boundaries were not honored, and where schedule chaos may have been an additional stressor. Even everyday products like bottles of cleaning solutions were labeled, "Darcie's room." Every day was like clockwork in Darcie's room: eating at a certain time and naps never off schedule. My communication with Richard had mostly stopped due to his controlling nature. He was so unpredictable! In fact, one Saturday night my neighbors found Richard on their back deck spying on me! They described his eyes as being dilated, possibly because he was on something. They ordered him to leave.

When our children were in the fifth and third grade, respectively, I baked some cornbread to take to the Stew and Cornbread Day. As I passed my ex in the parking lot, he barked, "Chicken legs!" Totally uncalled for, but just another instant put-down like he had done for years when we were together.

A Big Fright

I was told that years before there had been a lady at the center named Linda, and the church family really helped her a lot. She had two sons and had also been in an abusive marriage. When she would come into the center with bruises on her face, the ladies got make-up and gently applied it. When she came to church, men walked her to and from her car as her husband sometimes waited in the parking lot in his car, just part of his stalking her. At one point, he took off with one of the children and hid him away at a lake property. The police finally got the boy back. Then a protection order was granted by the court, which he violated one day after work by hiding in her closet. She ultimately remarried, got full custody, and they're all quite happy today.

I remember thinking, I don't think I could go through that, until it happened to me. Hard to believe. Richard had the kids one weekend, and they went to my brother's home. I went to church that Sunday, and we sang songs like "Whom Shall I Fear?" I was just beginning to feel strong in myself again. "I am not afraid of you!" I said when Richard called one night.

"Oh yeah?" he replied menacingly.

My children didn't come home that night. I didn't know what to do and was almost paralyzed with fear for the next few days. When I called my attorney to find out what I could do, I found out that he had dropped my divorce petition without any word to me whatsoever. Richard was free to take them, according to his attorney.

Wow, was that a heart breaker! I was in a panic. They were obviously missing school, their familiar environment and routine, and reassurance from their mom. With no information about where they were, what was happening, and what might happen next, my mind struggled to feel any optimism. There were missing children's posters up, with my children's faces on them. I was so distraught and sick to my stomach, and I could barely walk. I stayed on the couch at home and tried to make sense out of this, figuring out what I could do.

I knew in my mind that Richard wouldn't hurt the children, but it was complete anguish not knowing where they were.

What a disruption in our lives! I felt like the closer I got to the Lord, the stronger the attacks I had to endure.

Well, the judge was not happy that my children were missing school, so he ordered Richard's attorney to get them back home at once, and a hearing in court was scheduled for the following week.

My mom came to stay with me during that time, and I started a journal on my feelings. Because I missed work for a week, being unable to function, my church family took up an offering for me. It was such a sweet gesture and much needed. Yet I had such a sick feeling, I worked on the same church campus that had my children's faces plastered everywhere. While my mom was staying with me, time just stood still. Neither of us had any preparation for such an event, if anyone ever does. All this left both of us feeling simply helpless. Mom played the guitar and helped me fix our meals. I called the local TV news and got my children's story on the air. To this day, my heart gets numb when I hear an Amber Alert. I know that feeling all too well.

Although I was certain that my ex had my children because of the testy phone call that preceded their not coming home, I still called anyone I thought might know, including Richard's parents in Indiana, who initially didn't answer my calls. A few days later, Richard's stepdad finally answered the phone, and asked, "What the hell is going on in Georgia?" He told me that the kids were with extended family there in Indiana.

I thanked him, as that provided me with some peace of mind. In fact, Richard had taken them back to his sister's house in Indiana and had them there for thirteen days, but all that time, I didn't know where they were. The judge for my case issued a warning to Richard, through his attorney, that because the kids were missing school, they had to be returned within a certain time or an arrest warrant would be issued.

I could have filed a criminal complaint, had my attorney not dropped the divorce petition with the court without my knowledge. He had been paid in full by my parents. Legal malpractice, but what was an impoverished single mom to do about that? I didn't even find out about this until we were back in court again. There I was, learning yet one more disturbing thing. I felt so numb and helpless in a system that was supposed to protect me.

My ex got away with no retribution, legally or financially, for kidnapping the kids. A move made simply to retaliate for my saying I was no longer afraid of him. That new status, long overdue, must have really threatened his selfish, controlling mindset.

Ms. Barbara finally called me one day and said, "Why don't you come back to work and keep busy?"

So I did. My mom went with me, and I must be honest, I couldn't believe my life was turning out like this. All because of one person and the bad choices he had made. In retrospect, Richard ultimately damaged every life he touched. I never told anyone I was abused, but truly I was. You don't believe it is abuse until you begin to heal. Being controlled is the hardest part for victims to become fully aware of and admit. We begin to disavow and retrain our minds to not care about what the predator is thinking or doing. I was so thankful that Mom currently was a supportive figure for me. She left her business to come and help me for a short while, and I'll never forget it.

After thirteen days, the police escorted my children back to me. The kids seemed fine, but remember, there were no cell phones back then, so they couldn't have just called me. I held them gently in my arms and told them, "It's never okay for me not to know that you're okay. I worry about you so much when I'm not with you." The next day, I got them back on a schedule and into our normal routine again. Later while working in the toddler room, Ms. Barbara came in with tears in her eyes. She said, "I'm so glad the children are back home."

My mom returned to her normal life in Indiana as well. Mom and Dad weren't quite retired yet, but soon they did.

They had worked so hard for this season in their lives. They bought a motorhome and traveled and enjoyed seeing the beautiful United States. My kids spent two weeks during the summer with them in their retirement in Tennessee, and my brother's kids went there as well. But while their lives were pretty normal, daily life for my children and me remained a struggle in a lot of ways.

Ten years after the divorce, childcare issues, financial strain, and little emotional support still made life difficult. My parents were only a four-hour drive away, and when they did visit, they parked their car in my garage out of concern that my ex might sabotage their Crown Victoria. Other forms of support, such as phone calls and letters, seemed a little rare, in terms of what my needs were. I just needed occasional straightforward good words.

For many years while our lives were in survival mode, my kids wore hand-me-downs with no amenities, eating out, or vacations. I also had to scramble to find affordable but responsible babysitters to cover my evening shifts.

Even though my kids were returned, and I knew they were all right, daily life remained a struggle. It was much more stressful when they weren't close by, such as when he had them for weekends and summers, as nothing had changed legally. I didn't have the money to dote on the kids, so they weren't dressed in the best clothes. I found a consignment store I liked though and would take in old clothes to get some newer pieces. I remember my children loved a doctor who at one time had cried at their appearance because they were clean but not nicely dressed.

On Wednesday nights, we stayed on campus and went to Bible study groups, one for adults, and one each for girls and for boys. I was growing a lot spiritually at that time. I spent time in the Word when the kids were sleeping.

One weekend, when Richard had the children, I went to the campus to paint the toddler room. It was a great way to give back. The walls were pretty marked up by the kids, and I felt honored to do it. I had been moved up to the toddler room, so I wanted it to look fresh. I also enjoyed getting construction paper and putting names on the cubbies, personal holders for each kid's supplies. They were simple tasks and pleasures, but very meaningful to me, bringing a sense of responsibility, order, and accomplishment back into my life.

There was a little girl in that class whom I love dearly. She would run in to hug me every morning. Yet she did have an annoying problem of biting others. One day she bit kids thirteen times, so we talked with her mother, who said to let one of the children bite her back. That's what we did, and it worked! For once, the little girl understood how much a bite hurt. That was the end of that problem, leaving her totally adorable.

I then got moved to the kitchen because Ms. Melda was undergoing cancer treatments. This was not a wealthy center, because its mission was an outreach of all manners, including feeding the hungry, counseling, and classes for every age. So the commercial refrigerator was purchased through Ms. Bunnie, the pastor's wife, doing book work and laboring long to pay for it. I was honored to have the job title of daycare cook, learning how to prepare meals in large quantities. Cooking for children is a bigger task than you might think. Menus have to be made weeks in advance in order to know which ingredients will be needed so they can be ordered and delivered on time. Sometimes I closed the door to the kitchen and played my praise and worship music quietly. I loved it, and it gave me great peace.

Working in the kitchen also helped me run a better kitchen at home. I was allowed to take leftovers for myself and my kids so we could eat them for dinner. It did help keep our costs down. I really was in the presence of some spiritual giants. When I attended the church on campus each Sunday, the praise and worship leader had the praise team start in the back of the sanctuary and, with clapping hands, come forward with songs of victory, not defeat. They were ushering in God's presence, and when they sang, I felt as though I were in heaven. Sometimes in the worship, I could see a cloudy mist over us and I knew that was the Holy Spirit. Psalm 150:1, 6 (KJV) says,

"Praise ye the LORD, praise God in his sanctuary, praise him in the firmament of his power … Let everything that hath breath praise the LORD. Praise ye the LORD." (KJV). And Psalm 22:3 (KJV) says, "But thou art holy, O thou that inhabitest the praises of Israel." (KJV). Remember the mist that covered the tabernacle in the days of Moses? With sincere heartfelt worship, we can see that today. One song we sang was "I Went to the Enemy's Camp and Took Back What He Stole from Me." Another had words like, "If Christ be for you, who can be against you?" Gradually, I found out more about spiritual warfare and realized that indeed I was in a war, and I had been held captive for a long time. In some ways, I was only coming out of this by fits and starts, having been so controlled and lacking needed support for years. Even now, it's hard to look back and realize how many people knew of our situation and had the means to help in various ways, but chose not to, never to explain their withholding. I never experienced envy of anyone else's situation. I simply needed necessities and security for my children and myself. Another thing that changed for me was my desire to be talked to with respect and dignity. I didn't want to be talked down to anymore or feel like I was less than anyone else. At the center, everyone called each other Ms. Kathy and so on, always respectful and polite. I had had enough insults to last a lifetime, so that was a welcome change.

I came to realize that respect should be expected. I think that ties in a lot with boundaries and attitudes and setting them clearly in relationships. When boundaries are not reasonably defined, they can be intruded upon by thoughtless people who take advantage of demoralized, frightened, or confused people.

The Fatherless and the Widow

After doing research in the Scripture, I wanted to know God more and what's important to Him. I also wanted to know why in the world God would get involved with me.? Now you may think my children weren't fatherless, but they were. Richard was very undependable and followed through with very little. He said odd things that puzzled the kids. He sometimes said mean things, without provocation. It was common for him to not show up at scheduled times or to drop them off later than expected without calling. That certainly affected me. It rattled me with worry! Sometimes he brought them back early from summer visitation, with no notice that they were coming. Richard also gave me no help with providing clothing, shoes, or school supplies, which were very expensive. I remember how hard it was trying to start saving for the kids to go back to school, one of the most expensive times of the year.

If you know of a child with divorced parents, or perhaps an orphan that you see struggling, please try to see them the way that God sees them. Maybe you can help them out. Remember that widows often need help too.

My son once said of his dad, "He's like a turtle—make it to the water and you're good," meaning once brought into this life, it was up to the little ones to make it, like newly hatched turtles somehow getting to the water, parents not involved. How sad.

Having children is a lifetime commitment, and we should all take it seriously. The bottom line is, God knew I didn't have a covering, a shield from the storm, and now I feel He placed me under His covering. A backstop, if you will. Here are some verses I looked up, which shows how very serious this is to our God. It started in the days of Moses, with God delivering the children of Israel.

Isaiah 1:17: Learn to do well, seek judgment [justice], relieve the oppressed, judge [defend] the fatherless, plead for the widow. (Isaiah 1:17 KJV).

Zechariah 7:10: And oppress not the widow, nor the fatherless, the stranger, nor the poor; and let none of you imagine evil against his brother in your heart. (Zechariah 7:10 KJV).

James 1:27: Pure religion and undefiled before God and the Father is this, to visit the fatherless and widows in their affliction, and to keep himself unspotted from the world. (James 1:27 KJV).

I wonder how many times we miss a blessing by walking right by those who are hurting. Or because we don't see the needs of others or simply aren't concerned about their well-being. They miss out; we miss out. We should be like the Good Samaritan who didn't walk around or otherwise avoid the injured man he encountered in his journey. Instead, he bound the man's wounds and took him for continued help at an inn, leaving a donation for the innkeeper to continue the care he had started. The Samaritan wasn't obligated, but he saw the need, and he just did the right thing.

Even a youngster in grade school can discover this wisdom, and yet it can be forgotten over time, and elude even a "sophisticated" and seemingly successful adult, who may be distracted by their own chasing of worldly validations. When they are gone, the world will hardly miss them. Opportunities to have made a real difference to those who needed a kind word or a few minutes of intervention didn't just happen, for no good reason.

Yet often some people get help directly from the Lord, even in these modern times. He works in creative, often subtle ways. Be watchful and expect to see His caring and healing ways, sometimes delivered through the actions of acquaintances, or strangers who have no compelling reason to offer themselves, but they do, and the transaction is a dual blessing.

Wow, did you get that? That's why the Lord got involved with me, and my children. He understood how hard it is for us single mothers and fatherless children. This starts off biblically when Moses was delivering the children of Israel and goes all the way to the other end of Scripture in the book of James, written by Christ's own brother. ([See the scriptures listed in the last chapter.)]

If we really search the Scripture, we find the reason the church was started was to make sure all had enough and had a reasonable and meaningful life without unnecessary suffering. Read that last sentence again. Let it long reside in your mind. We need to bring this legacy back into our churches today. A small gift card during back-to-school time, or a new outfit for a child, truly means so much to someone who is struggling. We can't forget these precious people, and who they are to God Almighty. We are placed here to do His will, if only we read and see or hear and understand.

I remember a staff person at church giving me a bag of clothes and hairpieces like scarves and barrettes. I felt like it was Christmas! I got home and took my time unpacking the bag to see what items we could use. What a wonderful feeling! Because we were still struggling financially, it really helped. Just little things! Don't underestimate the value of even these modest things.

My Four-Hour Visit with Jesus

After about a year and a half of working in this ministry, my daughter began having problems breathing while asleep. She would snore and breathe out of her mouth only. So I took her to the ear and nose doctor, and he told me she needed her adenoids taken out, as they were obstructing her breathing. She had surgery and everything was fine. Her breathing was much better. She was back to herself in a few days and returned to school.

While I was at work, Ms. Barbara informed me I had a phone call. It was the surgeon's office. I was told that a series of tests needed to be run on my daughter. We'd been so relieved to get through this recently, and now there was uncertainty facing us again, and probably more costs financially. Without going into details, there were ominous implications about what might have been causing more health issues, possibly quite serious, for my beautiful daughter, which really rattled me. So I asked if this was necessary, and was told it was.

I remember getting so upset. "Lord, I have done everything you have required of me," I prayed. "I'm in your Word a lot. I take care of children of low-income families. I just had my children returned from my controlling ex-husband. And now this. Lord, why? When is the suffering going to end? Haven't we been through enough?"

I went to the center and told other staff I wasn't sure what to expect, but that I needed prayer. Later that day, Ms. Bunnie, the pastor's wife, came in and said, "Would you like me to go with you?" She apparently had picked up on how panicked I felt.

"Thank you so much, Ms. Bunnie, but I think we'll be okay."

As I closed the daycare door and walked out to pick up my daughter from next door, Ms. Bunnie called a caution to me, "Guard your heart." She meant that I should keep from blaming the Lord.

I knew those words were from our Lord, and as I signed my daughter out and we left for the hospital, we both were calm. I explained to Beth that the specialist we were referred to needed to check a few things and we would be fine. But I had trouble finding the doctor's office, due to anxiety, even though I had mapped out our destination.

"Guard your heart."

Ms. Bunnie's words played through my mind continually as I watched Beth lying on the examination table. She looked so young and helpless. But I reminded myself that God was watching over her. "I don't want to disappoint You, Lord," I prayed. "I don't want to be like the ungrateful Israelites. Help me to put You first."

To my relief, Dr. Ray pronounced her well enough to leave, so I took my daughter home without discussing the incident.

Later that night, I scurried the children to bed and went downstairs to get into the Word. "You are everything to me," I told Jesus. "I owe You so much for what You brought me through and out of."
As I snuggled under the covers to pray, I fell asleep. I like to fall asleep while praying. Something woke me up a few hours later. I glanced at the clock to see that it was midnight. I gasped in delight as I felt an overwhelming sense of pure love wash over me. Suddenly a veil of light draped my bed. The veil kept unrolling like an ephemeral scroll as it encompassed my bed. It was so majestic!

My soul was thrilled when glistening white lights began flashing down on me one after another. As the love and lights continued, I just lay back and soaked it all in. It seemed that I was floating on air. The comfort and acceptance I felt couldn't be described by any dictionary. I basked in the refreshing spirit. I had no doubt that Jesus was visiting me to confirm that I was His child and that I was important to Him. I had passed the test by putting my trust in Him—even when my own flesh and blood was in danger. Although no words were spoken, they weren't needed.

I remember thinking that if I didn't have children, I would have wanted to go to heaven that night. As Paul states in the scriptures, "We cannot comprehend what the Lord has in store for us."

Mansions? Yeah, I'm in.

When the lights faded away, I looked at the clock again. It was 4:00 a.m. I was so excited I could hardly breathe! I had just experienced four hours with Jesus! I lay there trembling in anticipation of telling my friends at the Lithia Center all about my encounter with Jesus. I couldn't wait to get to work! I couldn't get the children up fast enough the next morning. Wait until I tell Ms. Barbara!

After I got to the center and told her, Ms. Barbara just smiled a big smile and reflected on how wonderful our Lord is.

Once I was back working in the kitchen, Ms. Barbara got a call from the doctor, saying everything was negative. It hadn't hit me that I must have passed a test, but later I searched the scriptures and found a few verses that said:

Matthew 10:37: He that loveth father or mother more than me is not worthy of me: and he that loveth son or daughter more than me is not worthy of me. (Matthew 10:37 KJV).

Luke 14:26: If any man come to me, and hate not [instead worships] his father, and mother, and wife, and children, and brethren, and sisters, yea, and his own life also, he cannot be my disciple. (Luke 14:26 KJV).

Family is to be cherished, but not worshiped.

Wow, those are powerful words of our Lord, and He is plainly saying that nothing, no matter how precious, is to be put above Him. Look also at the example of Abraham having to leave his family in obedience to God, and then being asked to take his beloved son, Isaac, whom the Lord had provided him late in life, to be offered as a sacrifice. I want to point out that in Scripture it doesn't say, "He was willing to offer Isaac because he loved God," but it says he was moved with fear and offered Isaac.

The angel then said to him, "For now we know you fear God, since you have not withheld your only son from me" (Genesis 22:12 KJV).

I'm so sure that Abraham dreaded every single step to the altar. His heart had to be breaking! He loved his only son, Isaac.

I can honestly say that I've been tested with my own daughter and delivered … in the twenty first century. Why do we place God in a box and think He only functioned that way in the Old Testament? Many understand that they are called to love, respect, and worship Him, but fear of the Lord too often gets pushed to the side. It sounds too harsh.

The gown I was wearing the night I was with the Lord is in a shadow box today, along with notes to my grandchildren. The gown is blue and green flannel, with a pocket inscription that reads "Forever Young." It was a night I will never forget and can never get out of my mind. I hesitated to share my story until recently, not wanting to exploit a very sacred moment in my life. I look at our world today and see people looking for answers through social media, celebrities, the royal family, the lives of the rich and famous, scientific theories, politics, and politicians. Our souls long for fulfillment, but our Creator made us for worship and fellowship with Him. And without Him, those needs will never be met.

My time at Lithia Christian Center was now coming to an end, as the Lord was taking me in a new direction. I had a class of four-year-olds in my last months with this ministry. Every class helped me to grow. Having structure again was somehow restorative for me. The whole time was refreshing while planning, preparing, executing, cleaning up, and being a role model for the little ones. My last class assignment dealt with more misbehaving toddlers, but I created new ways to keep their attention and give them gentle structure. There were more growing pains, but I felt ready for what God had next for me.

Rebuilding My Body, Mind, and Spirit

When I was single and in my early twenties, I worked for a marketing company and made very good money. Now out of the blue, I got a call about doing a marketing promotion on weekends, when Richard had the children. I was to stand at the entrance to a big box store for a grand opening and ask customers if they would like to sign up for a credit card and get a gift. I must have done well with the numbers because soon the manager was asking if I would like a job with the store itself.

At the interview, the human resource manager smiled and said, "We'll pay you thirteen dollars an hour."

I was so happy! I would have a nice income, plus benefits, which I needed for my children, and be able to get off the food stamp program. (I had to shop at night to avoid being embarrassed by paying with big food stamp coupons, which were so obvious. The more recent format change of this assistance to an electronic card is a godsend to the impoverished, who need their dignity to be left intact.)

I was still working on my memory and focus when I started this job. I had all of Ladies Apparel, including lingerie. These were some large areas, and I had a map to follow for how they wanted the department to look. With both children in school, I could just pay for an after-school program or babysitter. I worked from 8:00 a.m. until 4:00 p.m., so it really was a nice schedule for us. I was home in time for dinner and homework.

Again, I want to stress how I was growing at this time—stretching and being strengthened a little bit more and more. Having people on board who were helping me was so nice. It took a while, but I was finally getting the hang of it.

I had a dear friend, Mr. Davis, who helped me by cutting my grass every other weekend when I had to work. If I had the children for the weekend, he was more than happy to stay with them. He soon became like a grandparent in their lives, when none of their own grandparents were involved much at all. I could never fully express my gratitude to him, always bringing over Mr. Goodbars or homemade chicken biscuits made at a local gas station with a dining area. What a treat! That meant a lot to all of us. We still appreciate his kindness to this day. My grown daughter still speaks of him and his treats whenever she sees a Mr. Goodbar candy bar. Richard's housemate, an older guy named Mr. Hicks, had two elderly sisters who were wonderful to my kids. It took more worry off me because I knew when he and his sisters were looking after my children, they were in a stable environment. It was comforting to know that even if Richard didn't come home, the kids were in good hands.

On the other hand, my daughter painfully recalls waiting for her dad, never sure that he would show up on schedule.

I worked for the chain store for three years and started understanding how retail stores operate, with the various sections—: receiving, front end, backroom, and so forth—, and the department manager responsibilities. I was able to go in on an overnight shift and reset the whole ladies' area, walls, racks, new signage, everything that shoppers saw when they first entered the department. I felt so good about it, and it was such a positive growth experience for me.

Unfortunately, there was also a downside to the job, a painful one at that. It began with a couple of male bosses, who gradually began a pattern of obvious sexual harassment. Many years before the Me-Too movement, I had no one to turn to, and knew that human resources wasn't a safe place to register a complaint. These bosses knew very well that I was a single mom on a limited income, with limited prior job experience and no college degree. They knew that made me more vulnerable since I couldn't afford to lose my job by complaining about anything, especially about upper management.

After about a year of putting up with this hostility, I finally approached the female store manager, who, by law, had to document what I described happening on many occasions.

Things at work seemed to get better for a while, but then one morning, I walked in to find several store executives, all lined up, obviously waiting for me before the store opened for the day. There were five guys and the female store manager standing there. The men's mouths were contorted in an unnatural, sexually suggestive fashion. They all stood in a row, just staring at me, enjoying my discomfort. This was a group mimicking exactly what I had complained about to the manager. All I could do was pretend I didn't notice the vulgarity, clocked in as usual, and hurried to my section. I stayed in that area for the entire day, trying to make my day more normal and dignified.

So much for that day or those following, as this form of harassment went on for three long years. I stayed there because I had to have benefits for my children's insurance, and management knew I was in too precarious a situation to resign or take any legal action against their persistent perverted behavior. If I named the company, there is hardly a reader on earth who wouldn't be familiar with the brand. However, I regularly dropped by a local K-Mart when I knew the hiring manager was to be there, hoping for an opportunity to get another job in a respectful environment. Even though I had experienced harassment at the big box store where I worked, they did honor a request I made just after one Christmas. I asked if I could please have one of the fully decorated shrink-wrapped Christmas trees, from a number being given away to local charities. Someone from my church came in a pickup to carry it to its new home at the center, where it looked so stately. It was an artificial tree with very expensive ornaments, so it could be used for many Christmas seasons. It made me feel good to give back to the center in some visible way.

One Friday night, many months later, the children's dad was supposed to have them, but he never showed up. Normally it wouldn't bother me, but for some reason, I had an unsettling feeling in my stomach.

The next morning while at work, I called Mr. Hick's house. He said he hadn't seen Richard in several days. That troubled me deeply, even though I had the children with me at the time. This wasn't normal behavior for him, as he usually called if he couldn't pick up the children that weekend. I kept calling to see if there was any word yet. Finally, I received a phone call from a hospital in Georgia. A nurse reported that Richard wanted me to know he was in the hospital, and to explain to the children why he hadn't shown up for them.

The hospital was in Atlanta, and I went to see him the following weekend. I walked in and was directed to Richard's room. There he was, lying in a hospital bed with a punctured lung and other serious injuries. He told me he'd been drunk when he wrecked a company truck the previous Friday night. That was the reason he didn't pick up the children. I guess he collided with someone and was thrown through the front windshield (obviously not wearing his seat harness). It was hard to believe he had survived that. Part of me felt sad and sympathetic, until it suddenly occurred to me that he could have had our children in the truck with him that night. They could have been injured or worse! Later after getting home, I tucked the children into bed. I had not yet discussed any of this with them. Then I called Richard's mom and explained that he was supposed to have had the kids that last weekend, and would she please be a concerned grandmother and have him sign the children over to me for their safety. She agreed to do that, and, fortunately, he agreed to that as well.

The reason I called her is that Richard and I had little direct communication, which made coordination of family life and other realities difficult. What kept me from trying to communicate with him directly is that whenever I did, he seemed to perceive that as an invitation to subject me to his compulsive need to control me. While I was staying at the Christian Center, Richard sometimes called staff members at home, and was so pushy that they felt harassed and, ultimately, began refusing his unpleasant demands.

When originally going through the divorce, I had received a protection order from the court, which is theoretically available to any party feeling threatened during a separation. However, it had expired, but by this time, I no longer felt I needed that protection.

Knowing all the problems Richard had already had and knowing he wasn't going to overcome them on his own, I withdrew some money out of my 401K and asked the attorney to make modifications to the original divorce terms. I could then move out of Georgia, with sole custody. I also agreed to drop the child support down from $700 to $400 per month. If an alcoholic doesn't seek effective help, there's often a downward spiral, affecting all involved parties who depend on them. This includes damaging not only the relationship with their children, but the children themselves, having witnessed those behaviors and unable to depend on a major figure in her life. Then when that person is no longer around, they suffer a sense of abandonment and the mixture of feelings that goes with that.

While pursuing full custody and still employed at the big box store, I began feeling I wanted another move up for my personal growth. I had always liked K-Mart and had friends that worked there when we were in high school. Maybe I could become a manager at one.

I did get my resume into the office of the district manager, and for the longest time, I politely called him regularly to see if anything had come open. I got to know him on a first-name basis and found that the position I would most likely qualify for was as an assistant manager.

Wherever the district manager was for the day, it was quite possible that I would show up, hoping for a conversation. One day about a year later, the phone rang, and I was asked to go in for an interview. I was thrilled! I told no one at my current store, not even my closest friends there. The interview was in a conference room in a fancy hotel in Marietta, with hors d'oeuvres and fancy soda drinks all over—I liked this already.

I was interviewed by a regional manager for K-Mart. He looked over my resume and liked how well-organized my current company appeared from my descriptions and thought I could bring more structure to the table. So he offered me a position as assistant manager and placed me in a three-month paid training program, with a benefits package that would start immediately. At the end of the interview, I was offered some fruit and vegetables to take home, which were left over from a conference and the interview function. My guess is that realizing that I was a working single mom, he probably figured we were barely making ends meet. A small gesture perhaps, but so meaningful to me! My memory of it is still vivid.

After working at the training store for a few weeks, I remember asking my manager, whom I knew to be a Christian, if he would pray that I got full custody of my children. "Of course," he replied.

A few minutes later, there was an overhead announcement that all employees not with customers or on a register were invited to the cafeteria for a breakfast made by management. So we didn't pray at that moment. I have a feeling he prayed about it later though.

My reaction was that the one-time meal event was my training manager's way of saying that we were valued here, not just as employees, but as people. I recall questioning positive comments at my new job. Was that meant as sarcasm? I would ask myself. I had been subjected to so much ridicule in the past that it made me second-guess genuine acknowledgments for many months.

Although most K-Mart stores are closed now, they were a huge help in my education of leadership, compassion, and in the restoration of my self-esteem. A coworker and an assistant manager from my previous store, followed me to work to ensure my safety.

This was a time when K-Mart and other retail chains were having challenges keeping up with technology. They were just getting used to new efficient tools like handheld barcode scanners for quickly knowing inventory and assisting in product orders, sales details, labeling, and so forth. I experienced this as an opportunity for more growth. Perhaps this was an example of my need to see challenges as opportunities, rather than burdens or tasks I might never master. And that was probably part of what kept me going, even though I had a social support system that was still incomplete. Opportunity could spell growth, and eventually recognition, which certainly wouldn't hurt my feelings of self-value.

My training program was at one of the most well-known K-Marts in Georgia, right next to one of the oldest Kentucky Fried

Chickens in the country. Locals called it "The Big Chicken" as it actually had a big chicken on the sign, whose mouth moved up and down! The training was very thorough, and I quickly learned every part of the store and how it operated. I started with customer service, becoming familiar with policies, operating the registers, and dealing with various return/exchange situations.

Next, I had to learn the pharmacy area and health and beauty. The gal working there was awesome. She knew where every little item was, and I enjoyed learning to restock with her and perform the duties of the department manager.

After that was receiving. This department was run by a girl who was strong and organized. She was known in the business for running one of the tightest back rooms around, with nothing out of place. And I mean nothing.

When the trucks brought shipments in, she worked them as fast as lightning. She definitely sweat while she worked (well, Georgia is rather humid), as well as those working with her. While the pace of work at K-Mart was brisk, what was refreshing was that there was a total lack of harassment and malicious gossip. In fact, there were actually kind words here and there, from management and coworkers.

At one point, my manager gave me a gift card for two nice restaurants. My kids and I hadn't been out to eat for so long, which made it a very thoughtful and impactful gift that was much appreciated! I was trying to be the best employee I could. However, I was still dealing with anxiety and short- term memory issues. Sometimes I distrusted my own memory and organization so much so that I often backtracked to recheck something that I had, in most cases, already taken care of. I attribute these memory issues to having been abused and traumatized for so long. As a manager, I closed the store at night. However, even months later, I never felt confident that I had correctly memorized the seven-digit security code for the front door. In the few minutes it took to reach the door, I usually turned back to customer service once or twice and rechecked the number. This is what a traumatized person often addresses for months or years, both residual anxiety and lack of confidence, possibly even impaired short-term memory. All this can interfere with confidently handling routine things.

At work, I had to understand product knowledge, especially in the firearms area in sporting goods. The seriousness of running this department according to various regulations and company policies, such as running background checks on everyone and examining identification media carefully, was all quite stressful.

Not only were there essentially no computers in the store, outside of the manager's office, but there were also no handheld devices available either, used in order to verify pricing, inventory, or point-of-sale transactions that affected inventory. So at that time, vigilance and intuition had to be a substitute for such technology in accurately filling product orders.

Nonetheless, the experience produced further growth for me, including improvement in my memory, which I had to rely on for multiple functions in order to keep the department in good condition.

Upon finishing my training, I requested placement in the store nearest to my home. I wanted to be closer to my children's schools.

I enjoyed working at that store because the manager was a Christian and was very kind to me. I had had fears of mistreatment and unfairness and mocking, which had occurred with my previous employer. I still had flashbacks to those difficult and unnecessary events from the other chain, which had almost demolished my dignity. But the respect and safety in the new environment helped me focus on the present and the much-improved work environment. On the other hand, my work days were long, and I often had to close the store at night. By the time I got home, my two dear children were usually fast asleep in my bed, where they probably felt most safe. My nightgown was usually laid out across the bed. My daughter often left notes for me about their day and how much they had missed me. A few of those notes are in the pictures below:

During this time, I kept calling the attorney to find out the status of my request for divorce modification. I finally received word that Richard had signed all the paperwork. I felt so much better and relieved after that. One major weight had been lifted from my shoulders. I worked at a store that was well organized and managed, but unfortunately, many K-Marts weren't, and only six months after my assignment there, the company filed for Chapter 11 bankruptcy. It was all over the news, so rather hard to ignore.

With so little seniority, my fear became that I would be replaced by a more senior employee from a store that was closing due to the corporate reorganization. This felt threatening to me, as the family insurance coverage depended on my job there.

I took my fears to the store manager, who set up a conference call. We were soon reassured that employees of failing stores were not going to be transferred to other sites. Our operations manager was able to secure a position with Walmart, which seemed like a more secure situation, and he asked me if I might be interested in applying there as well. While still working at K-Mart, I had considered selling our family home once the divorce modifications had been made after Richard's serious truck accident and DUI. I felt I could finally sell that one and get a house that was just mine. I put a deposit down on one being built, a charming yellow house with a pond next to it. After all these years and struggles, I was going to have something that I had worked for and had control over!

One day at work, I got a phone call from the realtor. "Are you sitting down?" he asked. I could feel my heart sinking as I anticipated really bad news. Richard's health insurance with his new company had not come into effect, so his $43,000 hospital bill had been placed as a lien on the house we had.

This scuttled my ability to finalize the purchase of my dream home. Back at home after the kids were taken to school, I had to unpack boxes, tears making it difficult to see.

At this point, I didn't know if I could get out of this lien. My parents came down from Tennessee, and we drove to the hospital where Richard had been and met with the business office. I put pictures of my children on her desk and said, "This is who you're hurting by charging me with
$43,000 and 12 percent interest, as proceeds of the sale of this house were set up as a trust for these children."

She said she understood my point but stated that it wasn't fair to the hospital if any part of the bill were discounted or written off, and Richard's name was still on the title to the house, which allowed them to go after it.

My parents and I returned to the house, and I made calls to other attorneys to retain better counsel. The first thing I let my new lawyer know was that I had trouble trusting attorneys after my last one dropped the divorce petition without even notifying me. He told me he wanted to earn my trust. We discussed a quitclaim deed, but the problem was Richard's name on the title when the hospital put the lien on it.

He talked to the attorney for the hospital, who turned out to be someone my new attorney had gone to law school with. I had had to live with this unfortunate stress for an entire year. Near the end of my training period, I got a call from my new attorney. He informed me that the hospital was going to drop the lien because it was never signed by anyone. So the quitclaim deed was filed and the house could now be sold without Richard's involvement and signature!

I listed the house again, and it sold fairly quickly, with the proceeds divided into thirds: one for each child in trust and one for me. My dad offered me a small lot he already owned in a little town in Tennessee. I could build a new home on it for $35,000. But at that point, I had a job I liked. And the children were doing so well in the local schools, not to mention that they had made lots of good friends they didn't want to leave behind. With all of this, I finally decided to apply to Walmart. I wanted to be with a company that was stable, especially needing the insurance for the kids.

I received a phone call to come in for an interview, which seemed to go well. A week later, I was asked to take a test and have a second interview. Within about a week, I was hired. Both my K-Mart district manager and the store manager asked me to stay with them. And I felt uneasy about leaving my associates at a store that had been such a good experience for my battered psyche.

Although the decision was difficult, I felt I would have more growth and stability with Walmart, even though they had become so large that I worried I might not have the personal attention I had received at K-Mart. And I also knew they had a policy of placing employees pretty far from home if that was to Walmart's benefit.

Nonetheless, I gave notice at my store, and started at the new company without any break, and with a commute substantially farther from home. Picking up the kids from school and lining up childcare had to be worked out all over again.

Computer-based learning was heavily used in my three months of training, and the pace was fast. They did have their own backroom personnel, so I no longer had to unload shipments from the supply trucks. I was then assigned to soft lines (clothing and accessories), and I did well because of my strength in that area.

I was still working on my memory and organization of thoughts, while I worked at Walmart. This was a district store, quite busy, with four assistant managers, two co- managers, and around six hundred associates during the Christmas season. It was quite a challenge to remember people's names, various codes, floor layouts, and other details involved in serving many customers each day while still complying with company directives.

For example, one lady purchased a sheet cake for a birthday party and returned only one slice. She then demanded her money back because it hadn't quite met her expectations. The rules said she didn't have to explain, and she chose not to.

Most customers were pleasant and reasonable to interact with, but there were exceptions. And we were always expected to be as polite and patient with them as with anyone. We had an older gal working the phones at the store. One day, I heard the managers making fun of her on their walkie-talkies. I went up to them and said, "Does that make you feel big?"

Later that night, I asked the district manager for a transfer. I needed to be around people that cared about their staff and didn't mistreat them.

A few weeks later, I was transferred out of that store and placed in a division one store, which is much smaller and has less to deal with. The hours at work were difficult for a mother of two youngsters, sometimes not getting home until 10:00 p.m. and then back at the store by 6:00 a.m. the next day.

Sometimes I didn't see my children for two whole days! I arranged for supervision by available neighbors, which I paid to look after them when I was working. Sometimes it didn't provide complete coverage, and my ten-year-old would put my eight-year-old to bed, then herself, often leaving a note about their day: "Thanks for working hard and providing for us."

Some nights I would come home to find them both in my bed. Perhaps their choice of where to start the night was an expression of their longing for their parent, and possibly worrying about her welfare as well.

I felt a lot of guilt at this time. I was away from home working long hours and coming home so tired.

I worried about my kids while I was at work, even though my daughter was now old enough to walk herself home from the bus stop nearby. And I had a babysitter in the neighborhood for my son after school, the mom of one of his school friends. This worked out reasonably well, although if one or both children were ill, I still had to show up for work. Sometimes both of them stayed home if only one was sick, but that was just one method of coping. Fortunately, they were good students, even though they missed school occasionally, and were without anyone to help with homework much of the time.

We were blessed with goodwill and good attitudes in our small family, and each did their best. I always worked one day each weekend, and the reliable neighbor mom provided thoughtful care. But when I was home, my children's friends would come over, and life was good, as good as we could make it at the time.

I didn't date anyone during these years, hardly having the time, energy, or courage to take chances on a new relationship that might—like the first—feel right at first, only to be ultimately revealed as not what it needed to be, leaving my kids and me getting hurt once again. Later when they were older, they thanked me for not having to deal with another person during those times in which survival and some confidence-building were so important to all of us.

When I look back at all the things we had to endure, I'm in awe. I remember lying on my bed after tucking the children in, and saying, "God, please give me the strength to make it through another day."

Usually during my lunches, I would go and sleep on the human resources floor until my break was over. Although I was always tired,

I felt like I wasn't doing enough, especially for my kids. If you know someone who is going through a divorce, please realize that kind words go a long way. Remember also that long after a divorce, life can still be difficult. Some single parents don't have the luxury of families or friends for emotional and financial support. It's shocking how some family members don't visit, don't offer help, and live as if they had no relatives. Some may be financially comfortable, have plenty of vacation time accrued, or be retired, yet they don't inquire about what someone in the family, or maybe in their business or church or neighborhood, might desperately need, and be so grateful for.

Out of sight, out of mind—not in their consciousness, nor in their conscience. "What? Me? Worry?" may have been the irreverent denial spoken by the star of Mad Magazine, but the ugly ridiculous reality is that it's sometimes the attitude of people otherwise seen as pillars of their communities.

It's as if they're thinking, If it doesn't benefit me directly, then don't expect me to help out my family or a neighbor, even though this is one of the two requirements set forth in Scripture for eternal life: "And thou shalt love the Lord thy God with all thy heart, and with all thy soul, and with all thy mind, and with all thy strength: this is the first commandment. And the second is like, namely this, Thou shalt love thy neighbor as thyself. There is no other commandment greater than these" (Mark 12:30–31 KJV).

I saw the Lord's hand every step of the way in my journey. Richard rarely sent child support; however, during those years without payment, I somehow got a raise. I continued growing in my Walmart career, and I found I could retain a little more information every day. Post-traumatic stress disorder really is something that happens to our brain and changes it. It could be from a family war or a military war, any demoralizing and trying situation that threatens one's very survival.

I still struggle with having a good memory. Sometimes I'm plagued with unwanted, vivid recollections of negative events that happened to me and that have affected my children as well. With every promotion I received, I learned to trust the Lord a little bit more. I look around at this world today and perceive how far we've gotten from Christ and His Word. We can't turn on our televisions without having sinful or irresponsible behavior, or what I consider plain filth, come into view. Often these programs are endorsed, joked about, or even glorified as the best our culture can produce to be shown in prime time.

How long will it be before we come back to the God who made this amazing universe and the incomparable planet we're privileged to inhabit? How long will it be before people recognize Him as the One who formed us out of clay and set up the stipulations for our lives with ground rules that enhance life, protect the innocent, and give credit where credit is due? As much as I love the Lord, I fear him also. But unlike my fear of Richard, and of his erratic, undependable, spiteful, and intentionally hurtful actions and non-actions, my fear of the Lord is based instead upon respect and reverence for His righteous authority and the wisdom of His laws and directives.

God has given us so much, our very existence, and the gorgeous complex world we live in. He requires much in return. We shouldn't only be grateful for His love and wisdom and capacity to intervene in our lives, but we should also acknowledge that He sent His Son to shake up a chaotic and confusing world and to provide direction and hope for those who are suffering.

He expects us to take Him seriously, as the stakes are high. We should fear unending separation from Him and His benevolence, if we adopt a cavalier attitude toward Him, His commitments to us and us to Him, and to those struggling with goodwill everywhere.

I would like to close this book by asking you to challenge yourself. If you know of a struggling single parent, why not reach out and be like the Good Samaritan who didn't pass by the person gravely in need? This injured man had been passed by moments earlier by both a "so- called" holy man, who didn't take any interest, and then by another, who didn't want to contaminate himself with one from a despised sect, perhaps oblivious to situations that aren't advantageous to him, as many people are today.

In Luke 10:25–37, Jesus used this illustration to show us how we're to treat and love one another, even when it's inconvenient or not in our usual role. Do you see people in need and just pass by? The hardest part of that story is that nominally responsible people passed by and went to the other side of the road to avoid something that could cost time, effort, or alter their coveted identity.

Too many Americans have such little financial reserves. Even those with jobs find it almost impossible to pay for repairs to vehicles that they rely on. While you should always be careful about loaning money, simply offering to drive them to work for a few days could represent a miracle to them. That would make you a Good Samaritan.

I now own a busy hair salon. I've got a regular customer who's homeless. He sleeps in his car with a large Newfoundland dog. He told me his church won't allow him to sleep in the parking lot. What's going on when we can't help someone who has fallen on hard times? Where is this man going to feel God's love? Certainly not from the all- about-me world. Come on, church! Wake up! How terribly tragic that an unbeliever overheard the man speaking and then asked, "Why would I want to be a member of a church?" Good question.

My prayer is that because you read this book, you will get outside of yourself a bit and realize we're the hands and feet of Christ. People in need will be delivered by your hands and feet if you agree to be a blessing by going where life may be uncomfortable.

I don't know where my children and I would be today without the Lithia Christian Center. Those people helped when I was in dire need. They never made me feel like I was an inconvenience or a bother. They loved me and gently encouraged my growth.

Here's the key: Helping is such an integral part of their lives that they didn't think about it. They were born helpers, never oblivious or too busy to perceive burdens as opportunities to do the Lord's work by assisting one family at a time.

Visiting Angels

Contrary to popular belief, I'm sure that not all angels are huge, sword-wielding beings. I know because I've been visited by angels that were more like the pictures people painted long ago of angelic little girls with sparkling white garments and shiny blond hair.

"Lord, surround my kids," I prayed one day when Mr. Davis kindly offered to pick my children up from school.

I could hardly believe it when they all walked into the house. A feeling of warmth and security filled the room. Then I saw them. I watched two child-like angels walking up the stairs with my kids! The angels disappeared, never to be seen again, but that gift gave me peace, knowing the angels were protecting my children.

That wasn't the only time I encountered angels. One night an evil spirit woke me. It hovered over me, determined to frighten me. Because I was growing in Christ, I had been battling Satan's attacks often. I looked into those red eyes and ordered him away. "I bind you in the name of Jesus Christ of Nazareth. I take authority over you!" I commanded.

To my relief, the evil angel left immediately. I began to realize that I had power as a child of God! Another night, I was having unspeakable nightmares. I woke, feeling smothered by an evil presence and realized that I needed to rebuke that old devil again. "I bind you in the name of Jesus Christ of Nazareth. I take authority over you!"

Suddenly, I realized I wasn't alone. To my right, was one of the most beautiful creatures I've ever seen! She looked like a golden-haired child, but I knew she was an angel because she glowed with a heavenly light. Even her light-blue garments glistened and lit up the room. I watched in amazement as she raised her right arm and disappeared into the ceiling. The evil presence evaporated. "Praise God," I whispered. It wasn't long before I was asleep— secure in the knowledge that angels were watching over my children and me.

I've had several supernatural experiences. One night when the kids were at their dad's house, I was praising God with all my heart and soul, when I saw an amazing sight! My clothes suddenly lit up with a brilliant white light. I can only describe it as magical! Maybe that was God's way of showing me a glimpse of what my heavenly garments will be like. I can't wait! I don't have a desire to grow old in

this life. I want to stay just as long as God can use me—but no longer.
I'm ready for my heavenly home.

Invitation to Know Christ

If you've been in bondage with the enemy, don't think he'll just allow you to pull out of his grip easily. He fights for souls, just like the Holy Spirit does. If you're caught up in pornography, drug addiction, alcoholism, sexual perversions, or any other thing that displeases the Lord, please realize that we have a forgiving Savior that loves you, no matter what you've done. He died on the cross for you. Turn to Him today and make Him the Lord of your life. I promise you'll never regret it!

I'm not going to lie and tell you that it'll always be an easy road, but it will be worth it. After living in this sinful world, you can't imagine the joys that wait for you in heaven! Jesus has allowed me small glimpses of that heavenly realm and, I guarantee, you don't want to miss it! That's why I wrote this book. I want everyone to know that God is real. He loves you. And He wants to be with you forever. It's as easy as sincerely asking Him to come into your heart. Don't worry about changing your bad habits. Once He is Lord of your life, you'll no longer want to sin. Again, it may not be easy, but it will definitely be worth it!

We know from Scripture that Christ died for our sins and came to redeem all people. We're born with an imperfect nature and make both small and large mistakes in this life. His blood will atone for our sins if we truly repent in prayer. Christ wants a personal relationship with us, and we get to know Him through the Bible. My prayer for you is this: If you don't know Him, repent of your errors and then begin studying His Word. Then find a good, local church that uses Scripture, to inspire you to grow in your Christian walk.

The KJV passages below give clues as to why the Lord intervened in my life in both subtle and obvious ways. He wanted me to reshape my awareness and devotion and to provide a better quality of life for my precious children, whose father was alive, but missing in action.

You shall not oppress any widow or orphan. If you oppress him at all, and if he does cry out to Me, I will assuredly hear his cry; and My anger will be kindled, and I will kill you with the sword, and your wives shall become widows and your children fatherless. (Exodus 22:22–24)

He executes justice for the orphan and the widow and shows His love for the stranger by giving him food and clothing. (Deuteronomy 10:18)

At the end of every third year, you shall bring out all the tithe of your produce in that year, and you shall deposit it in your town. And the Levite, because he has no portion or inheritance among you, and the stranger, the orphan, and the widow who are in your town, shall come and eat and be satisfied, so that the LORD your God may bless you in all the work of your hand which you do. (Deuteronomy 14:28–29)

You shall not pervert the justice due a stranger or an orphan, nor seize a widow's garment as a pledge. (Deuteronomy 24:17)

When you reap your harvest in your field and forget a sheaf in the field, you are not to go back to get it; it shall belong to the stranger, the orphan, and to the widow, so that the Lord your God may bless you in all the work of your hands. When you beat the olives off your olive tree, you are not to search through the branches again; that shall be left for the stranger, the orphan, and for the widow. When you gather the grapes of your vineyard, you are not to go over it again; that shall be left for the stranger, the orphan, and the widow. (Deuteronomy 19:21)

When you have finished paying all the tithe of your produce in the third year, the year of the tithe, then you shall give it to the

Levite, to the stranger, to the orphan, and to the widow, so that they may eat in your towns and be satisfied. (Deuteronomy 26:12)

Cursed is one who distorts justice due to a stranger, an orphan, or a widow. And all the people shall say, "Amen." (Deuteronomy 27:19)

You have sent widows away empty, and the strength of orphans has been crushed. (Job 22:9)

For when an ear heard, it called me blessed, and when an eye saw, it testified in support of me. Because I saved the poor who cried for help, and the orphan who had no helper. The blessing of the one who was about to perish came upon me, and I made the widow's heart sing for joy. (Job 29:11– 13)

If I have kept the poor from their desire or have caused the eyes of the widow to fail, or have eaten my morsel alone, and the orphan has not shared it. (But from my youth, he grew up with me as with a father, and from my infancy I guided her.). If I have seen anyone perish for lack of clothing, or that the needy had no covering, if his waist has not thanked me, and if he has not been warmed with the fleece of my sheep, if I have lifted my hand against the orphan, because I saw I had support in the gate, may my shoulder fall from its socket, and my arm be broken off at the elbow. For disaster from God is a terror to me, and because of His majesty, I can do nothing. (Job 31:16–33)

A father of the fatherless and a judge for the widows, is God in His holy dwelling. (Psalm 68:5)

Vindicate the weak and fatherless; do justice to the afflicted and destitute. (Psalm 82:3)

The LORD watches over strangers; He supports the fatherless and the widow, but He thwarts the way of the wicked. (Psalm 146:9)

Learn to do good; seek justice, rebuke the oppressor, obtain justice for the orphan, plead for the widow's case. (Isaiah 1:17)

Your rulers are rebels and companions of thieves; everyone loves a bribe and chases after gifts. They do not obtain justice for the orphan, nor does the widow's case come before them. (Isaiah 1:23)

Woe to those who enact unjust statutes and to those who constantly record harmful decisions, so as to deprive the needy of justice and rob the poor among My people of their rights, so that widows may be their spoil and that they may plunder the orphans. (Isaiah 10:1–2)

This is what the LORD says: "Do justice and righteousness and save one who has been robbed from the power of his oppressor. And do not mistreat or do violence to the stranger, the orphan, or the widow; and do not shed innocent blood in this place." (Jeremiah 22:3)

They have treated father and mother with contempt among you. They have oppressed the stranger in your midst; they have oppressed the orphan and the widow among you. (Ezekiel 22:7)

Assyria will not save us, we will not ride on horses; nor will we say again, "Our god" to the work of our hands; for in You the orphan finds mercy. (Hosea 14:3)

This is what the LORD of armies has said: "Dispense true justice and practice kindness and compassion each to his brother; and do not oppress the widow or the orphan, the stranger, or the poor; and do not devise evil in your hearts against one another." (Zechariah 7:9–10)

"Then I will come near to you for judgment; and I will be a swift witness against the sorcerers, the adulterers, against those who swear falsely, those who oppress the wage earner in his wages or the widow or the orphan, and those who turn away the stranger from justice and do not fear Me," says the LORD of armies. "For I, the LORD, do not change; therefore you, the sons of Jacob, have not come to an end." (Malachi 3:5–6)

Not everyone who says to Me, "Lord, Lord," will enter the kingdom of heaven, but the one who does the will of My Father who is in heaven will enter. Many will say to Me on that day, "Lord, Lord, did we not prophesy in Your name, and in Your name cast out demons, and in Your name perform many miracles?" And then I will declare to them, "I never knew you; leave Me, you who practice lawlessness." (Matthew 7:21–23)

And the King will answer and say to them, "Truly I say to you, to the extent that you did it for one of the least of these brothers or sisters of Mine, you did it for Me." (Matthew 25:40)

And behold, a lawyer stood up and put Him to the test, saying, "Teacher, what shall I do to inherit eternal life?" And He said to him, "What is written in the Law? How does it read to you?" And he answered, "You shall love the Lord your God with all your heart, and with all your soul, and with all your strength, and with all your mind; and your neighbor as yourself." (Luke 10:25–27)

Pure and undefiled religion in the sight of our God and Father is this: to visit orphans and widows in their distress and to keep oneself unstained by the world. (James 1:27)

Note: According to the National Coalition of Domestic Violence, twenty million people (twelve million are women) experience some form of domestic abuse each year. And these are only the ones that have been reported. The initial exit is the hardest part. There are temporary protection orders keeping the perpetrator from access to the victims, and houses available for them to hide, in almost every state. Please don't feel like you have no hope. Contact your local police department to see what options you may have.

If you need help now, don't hesitate to call the National Alliance of Domestic Violence: 1-800-799-7233.

Purple is the color for domestic violence.

About the Author

Cindy Medlock spent eight long years married to a man she thought would be an interesting, dependable partner. Her dreams were destroyed when he became selfish and unreliable. Although she wasn't sure she and her two children would survive, due to a lack of social and financial resources, she was led to the Lithia Christian Center in Georgia. While there, she encountered an incredible miracle that validated her undying faith in God!

Life wasn't easy for this single mom, but she was able to meet the challenges put before her because she realized Christ expected her to keep striving, even when she felt intimidated and overwhelmed.

The Lord has blessed her with a thriving hair salon in a small town in Tennessee, where she offers her services at affordable prices.

Before that, she had the opportunity to train women in her own licensed cosmetology school. She wanted to make it possible for people with limited income to learn a trade, empowering them to provide for their families.

Her ex-husband was diagnosed with depression for which he now takes medications. He also since has helped greatly with their disabled son when she desperately needed assistance. God has since blessed her with an amazing Christian husband who makes her laugh and enjoy life every day. They attend a spirit-filled, loving church.

Cindy hopes to become a role model, inspiring people to do their best every day, the way the true Christians at the Lithia Christian Center inspired her.

Cindy has recorded two Christian music CDs and enjoys singing and speaking in churches of all denominations. If you would like to invite her to inspire your congregation with her encouraging message and songs, you may contact her through email at cindymedlock30@gmail.com or by mail at

Cindy Medlock

250 Memorial Drive

Paris, TN 38242